Lucid Intervals

For Hot Crawley — with warm good wishes —

Robert Steed

11/84

Lucid Intervals

by ROBERT L. STEED

illustrated by JACK DAVIS

MP

Mercer University Press/Macon, Georgia 31207

ISBN 0-86554-064-0

Lucid Intervals
copyright © 1983
by Mercer University Press

All Mercer University Press books are produced on
acid-free paper that exceeds the minimum standards set
by the National Historical Publications and Records Commission.

The works contained herein have appeared previously in various publications, including *The Atlanta Constitution, The Atlanta Journal-Constitution, The San Francisco Examiner, The Atlanta Lawyer, The Younger Lawyers Section Newsletter of the State Bar of Georgia*, and *National Comment*.

LIBRARY OF CONGRESS CATALOGING IN PUBLICATION DATA

Steed, Robert L., 1936-
  Lucid intervals.

  I. Title.
AC8.673   1983   081   83-699
ISBN 0-86554-064-0

Table of Contents

About the Author

Robert Lee Steed was born on November 20, 1936, in Augusta, Georgia, under mysterious circumstances. The mystery is that neither Steed nor historians can explain what he was doing in Augusta at the time. Steed claims he can't remember and the historians say they don't care.

At least one biographer contends that Steed's family was there having fled their ancestral home of Bowdon, Georgia, because of religious persecution. It is a fact that they were members of a now defunct religious sect known as Vichyssoise Baptists who believed that salvation could only be achieved through fasting, hip baths, and washing each others feet in cold potato soup.

In 1948 he and his family returned to Bowdon where he began a "serious relationship" with the person who became his wife and who is variously described in this collection as "my first wife," "my aging wife," "a dark, severe woman later identified as my wife," and "101 pounds of grit, gristle, and ingratitude."

Steed attended Mercer University which he contends was originally founded "as a refuge for students who were too poor to go to Emory and too proud to go to Georgia."

He claims to have heard Willie Nelson perform on the south lawn of the White House, seen a World Cup Soccer Match in Mexico City, and met Ali MacGraw on an airplane trip to New York. The editors of this collection have not been able to verify any of these claims.

He and his first wife have three children (though in late 1979 he confessed to her that she was not their real mother). They live in Atlanta where he is a member of a law firm which prefers not to be publicly identified.

The works contained in *Lucid Intervals* have appeared in various publications including *The Atlanta Constitution, The Atlanta Journal-Constitution, The San Francisco Examiner, The Atlanta Lawyer, The Younger Lawyers Section Newsletter of the State Bar of Georgia*, and *National Comment*.

About the Illustrator

Jack Davis grew up in Atlanta with a notorious group—later characterized as the "Buckhead Boys"—which included William Emerson and James Dickey. He attended the University of Georgia and the Art Students League of New York. During his career as an illustrator and cartoonist he has spanned the world for *Mad Magazine* and continues as one of *Mad*'s regular and most popular contributors.

His illustrations and cartoons have included advertisements of all descriptions, movie posters, record covers, Topps baseball cards, books, including a classic collection of humorous stories by William Price Fox, magazine and magazine covers including *TV Guide,* and, at last count, thirty-six covers for *Time.*

An avid University of Georgia football fan, Davis is the creator of the belligerent and zany-looking bulldog featured

on billboards, athletic programs and other UGA paraphernalia.

He and his wife, Dena, live in Hartsdale, New York. They
have two grown children.

Preface

Year after year a constant stream of people urge me to abandon the law practice and take up writing full time. Only the fact that all of these people are either my law partners or clients keeps me from putting pale thought to vivid action.

On launching a collection of this nature, self-introspection and the clamorous curiosity of a growing literary following demand an answer to the obvious question: "Why bother?"

It has been suggested that the artist himself is the poorest choice to explain his art or the motives for it. As a great philosopher once said (I think it was either Saint Francis of Assisi, Arthur Schopenhauer, or Merv Griffin), "The artist himself is the poorest choice to explain his art or the motives for it."

Having been thus disqualified myself, perhaps the keenest available source for that truth is my faithful marriage companion of twenty-five years. When asked by an awed reader as to why I devoted the time, the energy, the unremitting dedication to writing the columns collected here, she, with the uncon-

scious insight so often found in those who live in close prox-
imity to genius, said "I think he knows that it's an easy way to
get a picture of his big fat head in the newspaper."

—RLS

Dedication

To Lu—who has stood steadfastly by my side for almost twenty-five years, offering virtually no encouragement, and who is the unwitting inspiration, serene victim, and much-adored object of a great deal of what follows.

Jogging Your
Way to Boredom

If there is any ordeal in the Western world as tedious as submitting to a jogger's long-winded account of the raptures of his pavement-pounding passion, I have yet to discover it. There obviously exists a standard requirement that those preparing to take up jogging must take a stress test *and* prove that they are boring. Thereafter, they are entitled to stand by the clam dip at cocktail parties with a reproachful look and a glass of club soda, waylaying hapless fat people with harangues on physical fitness and the euphoric properties which result from their organ-jarring odysseys.

With practice they are reasonably easy to spot. They like to wear their old suits that look as though a family of gypsies just moved out; and their shrunken necks poke arrogantly from collars now so large as to resemble off-the-shoulder dress shirts. Their eyes are perpetually focused on infinity and burn with the zeal of recently converted Moonies.

If a middle-aged citizen chooses to menace traffic, neglect his business and cauliflower his brain by running through the

1

streets in his skivvies, it's all right with me as long as I don't have to hear about it. But one does have to hear about it, for there they are, everywhere, standing about like old ladies with photos of the first grandchild, ready to spring into the briefest conversational gap and tell you in grueling detail the step by step conditioning in their quest for a T-shirt which says "I Ran to Swainsboro and Back During My Lunch Hour."

Physical fitness, after all, is a matter of individual preference and definition. In my judgment, if a man's stomach measurements roughly approximate those of his chest (or, if he is forty or older, his shoulders); if his dewlaps cover no more than the top half of his tie; and if he is able to eat the planked seafood and an order of cinnamon rolls at Herren's and make it back to his office pausing only occasionally to catch his breath, then that man is in reasonably good physical condition. The joggers, of course, demur—loudly and at length.

Aside from being terminally tedious, they are humorless as well. At a recent convocation of that alcoholic approximation of a subway ride known as the Atlanta Lawyers Club, I had just managed to extricate myself from the Scylla of a monologue by a trial attorney as to the ever-stimulating intricacies of who entered the intersection first, only to find myself confronting the Charybdis of a jogger obviously bent on telling me how jogging had gained him physical and mental well-being and a mustache, and lost him 155 pounds of ugly fat (twenty of which were his and 135 of which were represented by his middle-aged wife whom he promptly shed after rediscovering his waist).

Taking the offensive, I immediately launched into an earnest monologue of my own about the salutary effects of watching TV while eating Cheese Nips and Malomar bars. He was stunned into momentary silence while I assured him that

3

although at first I was only able to watch thirty minutes at a time, I now had reached the point where I could sit through three hours at a stretch.

"It's tough as hell for the first hour," I explained, "but after that a feeling of release and euphoria comes over you, and you feel as though you can make it through the late news and sometimes even to the sermonette. My goal," I added, "is to get in as good a condition as the legendary Tom Watson Brown. He is now watching up to twelve hours a day on Saturday beginning with the Road Runner cartoons and going all the way through Live Atlanta Wrestling. Not only that, he couples the activity with such strenuous snacking that he recently received a citation from the Frito-Lay Company."

I paused as the jogger's eyes took on the glaze of a sugar doughnut. "I didn't know," he said blankly, "that you watched so much television."

I don't mean to imply that there is nothing to be said for jogging. There is, and Zell Miller recently said it: "They say that jogging will make you smart and I believe it. I jogged for three days and got so smart I quit."

(16 May 1978)

Democracy on the Run

Aside from the sheer dedication, heroics, and exhilaration from the front to the back of the Peachtree Road Race, the most amazing aspect of that massive, mobile, and self-propelled spectacle is how genuinely democratic it is. It's as though the Masters Golf Tournament invited the world to play and swarms of Avon ladies, plumbers, chiropractors, Shriners, and transmission specialists grabbed random implements and began whacking hell out of the Augusta National.

I should have realized that there was absolutely nothing selective about the event after seeing the prerace photo in the newspapers over the caption "Come Run the Peachtree Road Race with Atlanta Constitution Editor Hal Gulliver." The picture, which could have passed at Nuremberg as atrocity evidence, features the spindle-shanked Gulliver in a strap undershirt (reminiscent of what still passes for semi-formal attire in his native Valdosta) and a headband that he doubtless intended as an athletic affectation, but which I suspected as evidence that he had simply closed the car door on his head

again (a justification management has often used by way of explanation for his columns).

Notwithstanding this ample warning of the totally democratic nature of our swelling rite, I was simply flabbergasted (just the right word) by the spectacle. Having never seen it before, I expected something like a race or an athletic event and, for the first one thousand or so of the participants who moved serenely by, it thus appeared. But then! Great God! Around the bend a stampede appeared which would have convinced the unknowing that some sinister force had flushed everyone out of Marietta in their underwear and was herding them south with electric cattle prods. Twelve thousand sweating taxpayers huffing along in attitudes ranging from sheer desperation to low comedy.

There appeared to be four basic categories: the runners, the joggers, the lurchers, and, finally, the flotsam and jetsam division. The last category was by far the most colorful and courageous contingent. It featured grim and sweating housewives looking as though they had just gone over the wall at a European Health Spa and didn't intend to be taken back alive; geriatric marvels wearing T-shirts proclaiming "These are my real teeth too!"; a jogging juggler; and one particularly inspiring entry which looked as though 150 pounds of cellulite had been dropped from a high place onto a pair of sneakers—don't scoff, it was moving steadily. My favorite was one of those marathon walkers with a mincing gait which perpetually threatens to break into a full blown skip. I offered even money that he wouldn't finish the race in under fifty minutes, and was quickly countered by a swarthy citizen in mirrored sun glasses who gave nine-to-five that he wouldn't get past Pershing Point if any of the waiters at *Chez Quiche* spotted his syncopated strolling style.

7

It may be a race for the first hundred and it may be an athletic event for the next thousand or so; but I am convinced that Mel Brooks staged the rest of the affair and it is one of his best efforts. This is not to say that it isn't thoroughly worthwhile. It is a heroic challenge for every participant and a vicarious thrill for every spectator—not so thrilling, however, as to stimulate this flabby spectator to attempt anything more strenuous than getting up early to see it again next year.

If you haven't seen one, you ought to go while you can. Like hula hoops, marathon dancing and flagpole sitting, these things don't last forever. What passes for sanity inevitably— and for those who enjoy watching zany doings, regrettably— has a nasty way of reasserting itself.

(10 July 1978)

Fleetwood Mac and Brain Damaged Youth

A pressing and current question so often certified by parents, teachers, and sociologists is "Why can't Johnny read?" Volumes of speculation have been written as to why many of the SAT scores of graduating high school seniors fail to approach room temperature. What is wrong with our young people? Why can't they learn? The answer came to me at the Omni the other night in a flashing burst of intuitive light—brain damage from attending rock concerts!

I had no inkling that I was on the brink of scientific breakthrough when my aging but persistent wife cajoled me into attending a Fleetwood Mac concert with some other perpetually festive forty-year-olds. I was lulled into believing that the entertainment would be safe when she told me my friend Kimbrough had agreed to go. Kimbrough, whose personality is so bland he carries a piece of Velveeta cheese in his wallet for identification, was born into middle age and I knew his musical leanings were somewhere to the starboard side of Guy Lombardo.

My confidence was badly misplaced. It turned out that Kimbrough's cunning wife had told him they were going to a Mantovani concert. (He later admitted that he had heard of "Fleetwood Mac" but thought it was a promotion for some new kind of hamburger.) He should have suspected something when his wife, who always dresses him, brought him to the preconcert bacchanal wearing a cowboy hat, boots, and a Hartz Two-in-One Flea Collar. I began to sense something was amiss when I noticed that most of the ladies in our group were garbed in tank tops, high heels, and tight fashion jeans. A friendly observation on my part that they looked like the executive committee of the Villa Rica Junior League was met with flared nostrils and stony silence.

My apprehension took wing at the Omni when I saw that the average age of the milling throng was causing Clearasil to outsell Budweiser by a two-to-one margin at the concession stands. Apprehension gave way to embarrassment when I was the only one of our group to be physically assisted to a seat. The usher apparently thought I ought to be near an electrical outlet in case my pacemaker needed recharging.

Having missed the opening act, we settled in at intermission to watch the nubile postpubescents and their hirsute escorts scream and throw frisbees for the better part of an hour. On stage a group of grim electricians labored ominously over a set of amplifiers roughly the size of the Hurt Building (you can tell when a rock concert is about to begin at the Omni: as the amplifiers are turned on, the lights dim all over north Georgia). At great length, the houselights went down and a hush equivalent to a 747 making an unscheduled landing at Six Flags fell over the teeming crowd. We were then adjured to give a "warm Atlanta welcome" to the fabulous Fleetwood Mac.

Imagine, if you can, one of Hitler's Nuremburg rallies with electric guitars and marijuana, and you will have some small sense of the place. With the first eye-watering, ear-shattering chord, each of my internal organs went into a frenzy of sympathetic vibration which is only now beginning to subside. "Great God," I shouted to my wife, "they'd better get those kids away from the amplifiers!" Her blank look made clear to me that, except for lip readers, conversation at the Omni was over for the evening.

Fleetwood Mac, if you're interested, consists of a lead female singer in suede platform boots with a hairdo that looks as though it went best two out of three falls with a rotary lawnmower; a lead male singer who looks like Tyrone Power in drag; and a manic drummer who has to have been the menacing subject for the United Way poster which said "Support Mental Health or I'll Kill You!" The quintet is rounded out by a blonde lady who pummels the piano from a standing position, and a swarthy item on rhythm guitar who looked embarrassed about the whole thing. I sensed that but for the money, he would rather have been back at his old job as a lookout for a massage parlor.

As my group was leading me to our car following the show, I made out from Kimbrough's wild-eyed babblings that he actually enjoyed the performance; this confirmed my earlier diagnosis—his flea collar was much too tight. The doctors say that my hearing will come back in time, but what about those kids who were sitting down front?

(18 September 1978)

Biography of
a Soft Lawyer

(NOTE: For fifteen years Steed has paid tribute to his fellow attorneys by authoring capsule biographies which have been published in the Younger Lawyers Section Newsletter *of the State Bar. Reaction to these efforts by the biographees has been so enthusiastic that Steed for many years routinely had his wife start his car every morning. More recently, State Bar officials have furnished him a false identity and relocated him and his family to a small town in South Georgia where he now ekes out a living flim-flamming motorists on Interstate 75. The following effort, in recognition of the burgeoning feminist movement, features his first female victim who, until publication, was a lawyer in his own firm.)*

On March 4, 1945, a star in the feminist skies burst into brilliance in the small, dingy, snow-covered and heavily Polish mining town of New Cracow, Pa., when Ruth West Garrett was born. (A historical aside: the resourceful early Polish settlers came to New Cracow in the late 1800s and were the first immigrants in the United States to open dirt mines. The mines were clean, well run, and productive but soon closed because of what a surviving account of the settlement termed "marketing considerations.")

Little is known of her early years, but most historians attribute this to the lack of writing implements in Eastern Pennsylvania during that period. It is known that her strong feminist tendencies began to emerge during her early teenage years and in 1958 she attracted national attention when, anticipating the women's movement by ten years, she burned a training bra. The fact that it was being worn at the time by a competitor who had bested her in the Pennsylvania runoffs for the Miss Clearasil Pageant has caused some to claim she was stirred by motives less noble than liberation.

In her last year of junior high school, she came out foursquare for the women's movement and brilliantly articulated what was to become its central issue with her burning and now famous question: "Why have *we* always got to dance backwards?"

Admitted to Duke in 1964 as a Susan B. Anthony Scholar, she clung to her high ideals but avoided contact with the more radical feminist college groups of the activist '60s such as the now defunct "Don't Shave Anything League."

Although taking the moderate road, her outrage privately mounted as she learned of horrible discriminations endured by women lawyers of that day who were confronted with archaic rules governing courtroom appearances that generally prohibited make-up, culottes, and breast-feeding. Determined to right those wrongs, she entered Mercer Law School and was pleased to find herself in an atmosphere so forward-thinking and enlightened that restroom facilities were provided for female students. The fact that they were located in a nearby Amoco station and that a key and a small purchase were required to gain access did not diminish her appreciation of the sensitivity shown by the administration.

Following graduation, her icy professionalism, steely determination, high academic standing, and ability to tap dance and twirl baton got her a prompt job offer from the prestigious Atlanta firm of Whimper & Cavil. There she is one of eleven of their so-called "soft lawyers." (Ten are women and one is a recent Yale graduate who skips about the office and wears a scented handkerchief up his sleeve.)

While dedicated to feminism, she still manages to be the epitome of style. Many of her clothes are fashioned by the little-known New York Seventh Avenue designer, Yves St. Lipshutz, and others are from the world-renowned Loehmann's of Doraville. Her determination to advance the rights of women is tempered by a healthy (and some say job-security motivated) moderation; but even critics concede that her firm demand that all delegates to the 1977 Atlanta ERA convention be administered chromosome tests was successful in preventing many of the more radical elements from obtaining credentials.

With all this, she is a devoted wife, and mother of two. The story of how she manages her successful and loving relationship with her husband while putting in the two thousand billable hours required by her firm is beautifully told in her autobiographical sketch soon to appear in the *Georgia Bar Journal* entitled "Not Tonight, I've Got a Trust Indenture." She obviously cares for her two small children who are currently enrolled in the Joan Crawford Day Care Center, and tries "to see them whenever I can." The light of her life is her eight-year-old son, Bella Abzug Garrett, and she insists that his unusual name has resulted in no problems other than his strange tendency to wear a hat, be obnoxious, and twitch uncontrollably when Hamilton Jordan appears on television.

Those who think a big firm practice has softened her zeal for the movement need only note her recent reaction to a *Bar Journal* article by the legendary chauvinist, Tom Watson Brown. In the publication the portly pundit claimed that the efficiency of women lawyers is seriously limited by what he termed "inherently feminine characteristics" such as low hysteria thresholds, hot flashes, and the loss of incredible amounts of billable hours occasioned by their precise but time-consuming division of lunch checks. Ms. Garrett demolished Brown's sexist premise in a stinging and brilliantly researched rebuttal which revealed that Brown (1) is afraid of mice, (2) regularly pretends to be "in conference" while actually watching "As The World Turns" on his office TV, and (3) was the only Princeton draftee in the 1950s to fail a preinduction physical because of stretch marks.

Ruth West Garrett is truly a man for all seasons, and doubtless would have been elected to high office at the 1978 ERA convention but her husband wouldn't let her go.

(9 February 1979)

Ernest Tubb Lives!

How oft when in your recliner chair you lie in vacant or in pensive mood do those eternal questions flash upon your inner eye: "Whatever became of Ernest Tubb? Is he still alive?" Several Saturday evenings past, my answer to question one would have been: "He's propped up on the stage at the Great Southeast Music Hall"; and to question two: "The jury is still out."

"How," you doubtlessly are asking, "did one internationally known as a sophisticate, a watcher of public broadcasting whose personal library contains the complete works of Harold Robbins (several of which are in hardback covers) fall into such low company?" The answer is simple—a bad marriage.

My wife, whose deeply rural West Georgia origins are for the most part concealed, will occasionally reveal them in aberrant behavior such as: (1) planting purple thrift around our driveway; (2) whitewashing an occasional tree trunk; (3) crumbling cornbread into a glass of buttermilk and eating the unsightly result with a teaspoon; and (4) getting up a crowd of soon to be ex-friends and taking them to the Great Southeast Music Hall to hear Ernest Tubb "live and on stage."

Having conceived this notion, she straightway put thought to action by inviting our friends, the Allisons. They are usually available on short notice in that his disposition insures that they will forever be one of those couples who are asked out infrequently and then only because everyone likes the wife. He has one of those unfortunate personalities that must either be humored or lanced.

On the appointed evening his choleric nature, further aggravated by the fact that he was missing "Hollywood Squares," began to surface in the form of dark mutterings as our small party threaded its way through the pickup trucks and gaily painted vans in the Music Hall parking lot. In his customary loutish manner he began to grouse about the ominous implications created by so many Cobb County license tags.

At this point I interrupted to give him a well-deserved tongue lashing for what I considered to be his typically patronizing Atlanta view of our sister county to the north. I pointed out tersely and with some heat that just because a recent Cobb County poll had revealed that their most admired living female was Tammy Wynette; and just because the Cobb County Philharmonic was the only symphony in the country featuring a kazoo and a washboard and playing exclusively at K-Mart openings, this did not necessarily mean the county was the cultural Sahara many supercilious Atlantans presume it to be. After all, I pointed out, the Marietta Museum of Fine Arts has the finest collection of chenille bedspreads in the country.

Momentarily chastened, he accompanied us into the Music Hall that, we were pleased to find, had changed its previous all seating on the beer-and-wine-soaked floor format in favor of

rows of movie-type seats. An attendant explained that the old arrangement was abandoned after increasing numbers of patrons began to stick to the floor. The only flaw in the new setting was a nonfunctioning air conditioner. We joined the early arrivals in fighting off heat prostration and deodorant failure with copious quantities of beer while my wily wife, a veteran of countless sacred harp singings, quickly fashioned a fan from a popcorn box and serenely cooled herself pending the arrival of Ernest.

At length Tubb's Texas Troubadours, resplendent in pea green cowboy suits with darts flanking all pockets, patent leather boots, and ten-gallon hats, appeared on stage causing the moist loyalists to cheer and the ever-querulous Allison to speculate loudly as to how many polyesters had to be slaughtered to provide their costumes.

Finally, old Ernest "hisself" materialized stage left and tottered to the mike. I knew he had been a fixture on the Country and Western scene since gas was eighteen and a half cents a gallon and you got a place setting of cheap dishes with each fill-up; but I had failed to comprehend just how long ago that had been until I noticed that his guitar was covered with liver spots. It soon became apparent that the most important member of the group is the drummer who plays the drums, drives the bus, and beats Ernest on the chest during the breaks to get him ready for the next set.

But for all his years the geriatric marvel soon began to give us our money's worth; and despite the fact that the temperature in the auditorium finally reached sauna proportions; and despite the fact that midway through the show Ernest Tubb, Jr. (formerly the "Littlest Troubadour" and now a balding, bespectacled blue yodeler with a voice that sounds like a parrot being criminally assaulted by a much larger bird) came on and stayed much too long, it all came into country-clear focus at the finale when the "Tubb" wound up the show with a song he recorded in 1941 and broke onto the Grand Ole Opry stage with in 1943—"I'm Walking the Floor Over You." Even Allison's four years at Princeton were overcome and, obviously in the grip of long-suppressed recollections of his boyhood in Alabama's Hookworm and Pellagra Belt, he wistfully conceded: "That old gentleman can flat sing." He was right about that.

(11 July 1979)

Biography: a Lawyer with Richly Deserved Obscurity

In beautiful Southwest Georgia the lyrically named rivers Kinchafoonee and Muckalee, like legs on a pair of trousers, separate from a common source and flow softly southward to the sea bearing a rich harvest of raw sewage and industrial waste from scenic Columbus. At a point in the trouser-like configuration roughly approximating the crotch, lies bucolic Richland, Ga., where in 1944, Theodore Hester, then a relative unknown, was born in the living room of his parents' mobile home. (Although originally chartered in 1921 as "Bucolic, Ga.," the hamlet was aptly renamed during World War II after its leading citizens reaped huge profits from the sale of adulterated grits to nearby Ft. Benning.)

Hester arrived without medical assistance as the Cusseta midwife previously engaged by the family to be in attendance was being titillated at the time while attending a USO dance in Columbus.

Aside from a brief mention in the *Lumpkin Vindicator* of the fact that Hester was the first recorded breech birth in

Stewart County wearing glasses, the event went largely unnoticed. Even now his former townspeople are confounded by his success and fame. "Why," exclaimed erstwhile neighbor Gurleen Withers, Richland's acting Town Crone, "that little scutter was so ugly they had to tie a pork chop around his neck to get the dog to play with him." Another resident confirmed that Hester's mother regularly borrowed a neighbor's baby to take to church.

Subsisting largely on Double-Colas and "stump whupped" chitterlings, the boy's physique and eyesight steadily deteriorated. His rickets, thick glasses, and the fact that he wore a leather aviator's cap until he graduated from high school, gave rise to persistent postwar rumors that there was a Japanese holdout hiding in a nearby state park.

Despite early evidence of a personality that was destined to be terminally bland, the plucky youngster applied himself diligently at Richland's Johnny Mack Brown High School and in the twelfth grade qualified for membership in the school's elite Beta Club by demonstrating that he could read without using his finger. This and his election as second runner-up in the Senior Superlatives for "Best Personality" (he finished only a few votes behind a fern in the biology department) led to a full scholarship at the University of Georgia.

There the fact that he was the only freshman not invited to join a social fraternity assured a postgraduate invitation to Harvard where he was eagerly studied by a team of sociologists researching "Aberrations in the Egalitarian Order." Their discovery that he wore thick glasses and had no personality coupled with his native torpor (which they mistakenly diagnosed as intellectual arrogance) led to the automatic granting of a Harvard law degree.

A promising legal career in Atlanta as livery of a seisin

expert was cut short by the calamitous "Twig Blight" of 1971 and Hester was hired with some fanfare as administrative aide to a Georgia senator in what was then publicly denounced as a blatant attempt to woo the dullard vote. His employer's subsequent bid for reelection was thwarted when ERA lobbyists cannily persuaded the politically naive Hester to draft and introduce over his senator's signature courageous but unpopular legislation requiring sperm banks to pay interest.

Returning to Atlanta in disgrace, a disillusioned and bitter Hester vented his spleen by authoring violently antifeminist tracts under the psuedonym, E. Meriweather Merkin. His emotionally charged early works such as "Gloria Steinem Wears Boxer Shorts" gave way to the more mature and well-reasoned later articles such as "If Women Are So Equal, How Come Bella Abzug Is So Short?"

In 1974, mentally exhausted by his efforts, Hester voluntarily committed himself to a vocational guidance center where, after rigorous testing, an area of the law perfectly suited to his personality was found. He is now a highly successful municipal bond attorney in the prestigious Atlanta firm of Multilith, Quibble & Hedge.

(10 September 1979)

Why Are Dentists Free Men?

The question so often posed by philosophers, theologians, and deep thinkers everywhere is: "If, in fact, there is a God of Abstract Justice, why are citizens guilty of nothing more than chain saw murders, ax killings, and child molestation arbitrarily deprived of their liberty while practicing dentists are allowed to roam about as free men?" Well, maybe philosophers and theologians don't pose the question all that often, but it was damn well on the mind of this deep thinker last Monday as I drove slowly to a long-standing dental appointment.

The cause for this particular rendezvous with destiny was a previous visit some months earlier when, following a routine wash and wax of my aging molars, the dentist—idly engaged in computing his Mercedes payments with one hand and jabbing my bicuspids with the other—struck a soft spot with such vigor that to the vast amusement of his staff, I actually levitated.

"Well," he smiled as the concern over his next car payment disappeared from his face with the speed of an unarmed citizen passing through Central City Park, "that little fellow will have to have a crown. See my nurse for an appointment."

I explained patiently to the nurse that I would not be able to come in again for several years, in that my wife, who always accompanies me to the dentist, had a full schedule which obligated her to go from shopping center to shopping center making large volumes of unnecessary purchases. "Couldn't your mother bring you in?" asked the nurse, with what I thought to be a trace of sarcasm. I was about to point out tersely that my mother lived some sixty miles away when my wife, overhearing what she later callously characterized as "whining," came in and set the appointment. Observing crossly that many other forty-three-year-old husbands got to the dentist under their own power, she said that if she were unavailable for the duty she would "retain a Metro Ambulance and pay for it with my own money" (her "own money" being a much-discussed but never actually located commodity). With quiet outrage I set my jaw as firmly as my ample dewlaps would permit, and resolved to come in unescorted.

On the appointed day and hour, I strode into a crowded waiting room and struck a manly pose, confident that it would take some time to process all the cowering souls ahead of me. As luck would have it, the credit references on the early arrivals were still being checked and I was the first of our hapless number summoned.

"You remember Mr. Steed, doctor," said the nurse helpfully, "the one who always asks to be anesthetized before we clean his teeth." My attempt at lightening the atmosphere by requesting a blindfold and a cigarette went ignored as the doctor straightaway strapped me into a Naughahyde recliner and proceeded to explain in detail the impending carnage. At the first mention of "shots" and "drills," my medulla oblongata

quickly fused to the base of my skull and I can only remember thinking I heard him conclude " . . . and, of course, if the crack goes that deep, we'll need to remove the entire jaw."

Before I could raise a protest, he, his assistant, and a tray full of Black and Decker instruments settled comfortably in my mouth and he began a series of questions requiring essay-type answers. My last clear vision before locking my eyes shut in terminal panic was that of the doctor approaching, hypodermic in hand, with the stealth of a crooked veterinarian about to fix a horse race. The Novocain quickly spread from my jaw to the frontal lobes of my brain and cloudy, troubled thoughts ensued: "Will my heart stop when the Novocain reaches my navel?" "What is the incident rate of deaths per 100,000 during routine crownings?" "How do I know this man is really a dentist—anyone can rent some old magazines, a pastel smock, and smiley-face posters."

At length the good doctor, much in the manner of a calf roper in a rodeo, jerked both hands into the air and declared, "Done!" "Well," I observed as some feeling began to creep back into my nether regions, "that wasn't so bad after all. I didn't mind it a bit."

"You could have fooled me," observed the doctor. "You were in the chair an hour and a half and nothing touched it but the back of your head and your heels." I like a man with a sense of humor.

It is a good feeling to absolutely conquer an unreasoning fear and I have no dread at the prospect of going back for my permanent crown. But, after all, in this age of modern science, a temporary crown will probably last a good long while. If it holds up for about twenty two years I can get the permanent one paid for by Medicare.

(23 November 1979)

Canterbury Tales (X-Rated)

On the purest of intellectual impulses, I recently suggested to my first wife that we take in the movie version of "Canterbury Tales." Observing that the film was rated "X," she made some slighting remark to the effect that my interest was more likely lascivious than literary. Refusing rebuke in matters cerebral from someone who once assured me that most of Chaucer's work had really been written by Christopher Marlowe, I persisted, and last Friday evening we found ourselves in a queue along with a surprisingly large crowd of very strange people at The Screening Room. I suppose I shouldn't have been so surprised at the turnout; after all, there aren't that many opportunities to see an X-rated film in a movie house that (1) sells popcorn, and (2) doesn't rent overcoats.

Notwithstanding the merits of the movie, I would gladly have paid $3.50 just to see the crowd in attendance. I had expected a group that would appear slightly literary with prurient overtones—perhaps some hornrimmed, betweeded English professors from Emory, frayed at the cuff and lea-

thered at the elbow. Instead, what I found was a mob so bizarre in dress, manner, and appearance that the lobby looked like a cast party for "Bette Midler Meets The Village People." Of the first six couples in line, I was the only person without earrings. One fellow was particularly conspicuous in his fur chubby, jogging pants, and turban, but almost anyone in the crowd could have been picked at random from the bar scene in "Star Wars."

"These people are weird," said my wife. This observation, coming from someone who has established a growing reputation for weirdness herself, was a particularly telling communique. "Well," I assured her, "I'm sure they're harmless," but I nonetheless kept a weather eye on the crowd and a firm grip on my Milk Duds.

As we waited in the increasingly aberrant assemblage, we spotted a psychiatrist friend who was treating his wife and children to the movie. "These people are weird," he said pleasantly enough but stiffened when I observed that he was the only one in the crowd bringing his family to an X-rated movie. (I think the psychiatric association can lift the couch from any of its members who accompany children to a porno film.) Muttering to himself, he returned to his place in line.

When the early show ended, I noticed with a curious feeling of pride that the exiting crowd was not nearly as surreal as ours. A thought flashed across my mind that perhaps all of our bunch had been summoned by Diane Arbus for a group photograph.

For those who came to be titillated, the movie was a crashing bore. This month's *Cosmopolitan* shows much more flesh, throws in a new diet, and contains worthwhile articles on "Sex With Your Boss" and "Plastic Surgery: Should You Have Your Face Capped?" Aside from some slightly scatological moments, the scenes most obscene were those featuring the magnificently concupiscent Hugh Griffin, whose wonderfully lecherous leer alone could propel Hinson McAuliffe, axe-laden and frothing, toward the nearest projection booth. The scenes of fourteenth-century squalor, oafishness, and degradation were amazingly realistic (I later learned that much of that footage was shot on location in East Marietta), but as a porno film it was clearly lacking and certainly couldn't compete with the crowd that came to see it. I encountered my clearly disappointed doctor friend on the way out and we chatted for a moment until he paused to return the wave of a bearded, middle-aged chap wearing strap overalls, cowboy boots, steel-rimmed glasses, and a pith helmet. Sensing my eagerness at learning the true identity of even one in this outlandish throng, the doctor volunteered—"Friend of ours . . . English professor at Emory."

(9 January 1980)

The Female of the Species Caught in the Draft

The words "register young people for the draft" had barely issued from the president's mouth before the country was firmly in the grip of a coast-to-coast emotional spasm over the burning subsidiary issue: "Should the draft include women?"

Students at Yale, Harvard, and Berkeley staged their routine, outraged, and almost obligatory rant against the draft in any form. Response at the University of Georgia was mixed and, on the University of Alabama campus, where in late 1979 a handful of students staged their first rally protesting our involvement in Vietnam, there was thundering quiet.

The fiery, fulminating feminists, in a collective Pavlovian twitch, predictably demanded that women damn well better be drafted—right along with the men.

The reaction of the male chauvinist forces was just as predictable. "Do you really think," grouched one of my hard-line friends, "that the Marines could have taken Mount Suribachi if half of them had been wearing high heels?" Another apoplectic (and obviously married) ex-G.I. in gimlet-eyed rage

demanded, "How would you like to get into hand-to-hand combat and find that your bayonet was no good because somebody had been shaving their legs with it?" Thinking it prudent not to take issue on such an emotional subject with a shell-shocked former airborne ranger who has a bumper sticker reading "Nuke the Baby Seals," I, of course, agreed and added helpfully that I hoped the Department of Defense had considered the possibility that the noise from the hairdryers might well give away our positions to the enemy.

Carrying my research on this critical matter into my own home, I canvassed my family on the question. Their responses were uniformly negative. My wife said, "It's a ridiculous idea; PX's don't even have credit cards." My sixteen-year-old daughter termed the uniforms "icky," and my twelve-year-old daughter's chief concern was "Would they let you wear Add-A-Beads?"

Against this rising tide of *argumentum ad hominem*, my keen, objective, lawyer-like mind began to cut through the seething emotionalism and, with the cat-like mental agility for which I am widely known, I began to form a balanced, unemotional, and absolutely objective answer to the question of drafting women. The world, I imagine, waits breathlessly as we open the envelope and the answer is: "Yes. Definitely. Why Not?"

My considered judgment is that it would be a splendid idea to promptly declare war and immediately drop Bella Abzug behind enemy lines. If Congress refuses to go along with a declaration of war, I still think well of having Bella Abzug dropped, and while we are about it, they can throw in Kate Millett, Germaine Greer, Betty Friedan, and Jane Fonda. (On second thought, I might work out some sort of draft exemption for Jane Fonda as everytime I see her, lust seems to overcome politics and my reaction is not unlike that of the sheik in the old desert movies who, when he spies the scruffy Yvonnne deCarlo among the captives, points her out and says to his aide, "Clean her up and bring her to my tent.")

Swords into plowshares indeed; credit cards into draft cards is my battle cry. Harness some of that rampant feminist hostility. We added marijuana to the last war and lost it. If we add women to this one, we may never even fight it and, even if we do, it certainly won't start on time.

And while you are about it, Congress, don't stop with women. Draft children and pets too. Then, maybe, while they're all off making the world safe for democracy, I can come home to a quiet house, sit in any chair I choose, and watch whatever television channel I want.

That old jingoist Kipling figured it out a long time ago. Like any thinking husband, he knew and appreciated the killer rage that lies just below those soft and wonderfully contoured surfaces:

When the Himalayan peasant meets the he-bear in his pride,
He shouts to scare the monster, who will often turn aside.
But the she-bear thus accosted rends the peasant tooth and nail,
For the female of the species is more deadly than the male.

* * *

When the early Jesuit fathers
preached to Hurons and Choctaws,
They prayed to be delivered
from the vengeance of the squaws.

'Twas the women, not the warriors,
turned those stark enthusiasts pale,
For the female of the species
is more deadly than the male. etc., etc., etc.

Right on, Rudyard, and goodbye and God bless, girls; I won't sit under the apple tree with anyone else but you till you come marching home.

(7 February 1980)

Hell Hath
No Fury

While in the company of some fellow pseudointellectuals the other evening, engaged in nothing more mentally taxing than deciding whether to take another sip of whiskey and soda or eat some more peanuts (my wife gets furious if I come home with peanuts on my breath), the converstation took an interesting turn when someone raised this question: "What group, profession, movement, fringe, etc. is the most humorless of all?" Well, I thought, let the other pundits and savants labor over questions of global politics, aberrant economic theory, and nuclear proliferation, this is a real question, worthy of serious study.

Later in my chambers, I reflected on the issue and mulled over various prospects concerning which group has been thought lacking in a sense of humor. There came to mind lawyers, newspapermen, doctors, legislators, and (to coin a qualifying phrase right before your eyes) "last but not least," militant feminists (there may be something of a tautology there).

Fully cognizant of the verity of the old saying first uttered by some great mind (I believe it was either Aristotle, Descartes, or Phil Donahue) that "all generalizations are false, including this one," I nevertheless began to analyze the characteristics of each suggested group in terms of its sense of humor quotient.

Newspapermen and lawyers were quickly eliminated in that their high level of cynicism and constant exposure to the follies inherent in the human condition tend to cause them as a group to laugh at themselves and others. To be sure, there are pompous newspapermen and lawyers in ample number; but on the whole and as a member of the suspect category, I graciously decided that the humor quotient for both groups was reasonably high.

Turning to the medical profession, I thought that doctors had good balance and showed considerable humor in dealing with themselves and their patients. It would be dreadfully depressing business to be up to your elbows in some fellow citizen's viscera day after dreary day if you weren't able to crack a few jokes with the anesthesiologist and pinch a nurse or two while scrubbing up.

Some of my colleagues find doctors as a class particularly humorless, but in analyzing their complaints I narrowed the flawed areas to matters of economics and politics. Your average doctor, gay and jocund otherwise, will narrow his eyes, furrow his brow, and lose all traces of humor should the conversation abruptly turn to economics or government regulation. Doctors in a group tend to talk more about tax shelters than medical breakthroughs but, happily for us all, they are better at the latter than the former. (As one slick downstate realtor observed to someone who called asking about his inventory, "I've got good land and 'doctor' land. What's your buyer interested in?")

On the subject of politics and government interference, doctors are willing to believe almost anything and would not realize their legs are being pulled even if you pointed out a team of mules hitched to their brogans. At a recent cocktail party I was in the grip of a citizen I suspected to be a doctor (you can usually tell: they are ostentatious about wearing electronic beepers on their belts, and the younger ones, having noted that typewriter repairmen also wear beepers, will sometimes have stethoscopes hanging from their pockets to avoid any confusion). Just to bait the fellow and to keep him from launching into a conversation on the solemn wisdom of buying Krugerrands, I mentioned casually that I had it on very good authority that the Ayatollah Khomeini was not a real person but instead was a CIA plant in the person of former movie star, Gabby Hayes. Although he was initially dubious as to why the CIA would want to cause all this chaos and confusion, I managed to firmly set the hook when I confided that it was all part of a complicated government plot leading to socialized medicine. A look of great intensity and consternation crossed his face as he exclaimed "Right! I knew it!" and went away muttering to himself. I have happy visions of his wife trying unsuccessfully to convince him that Gabby, like Trigger, is dead, stuffed, and now in Roy Rogers's living room. But get members of the healing arts away from sheltering income and government interference, and they can be quite jolly and good company.

Legislators as a class do quite well, too. There is so much good humor when they convene that a friend of mine observed that bringing Ringling Brothers, Barnum and Bailey to town with the General Assembly in session was outright redundant.

Speaker Murphy is a master of the legislative craft but at the same time has a grand country humor that lightens and levels all House proceedings. Former legislator Roscoe Dean is unrivaled in telling wildly improbable stories while never cracking a smile. And one of the best kept jokes in the General

Assembly is the fact that the legislators have no serious intention of ever passing a gun-control bill but plan to keep introducing this legislation every year simply to aggravate John Crown.

By logical elimination I am left with the militant feminists. In recently sharing with the public in these pages my well-reasoned thoughts on the subject of drafting women, I incurred the apoplectic wrath of some of these dreadfully earnest missionaries and received such a torrent of venomous abuse that I break into an involuntary twitch at the approach of any female wearing a wide-brimmed hat. Following the publication of one particularly virulent letter to the editor (apparently the collective composition of six of the steaming sisters), a friend called to ask if I was worried about being picketed. "Pickets, hell!" I exclaimed, "I'm worried about snipers!" Now when I leave the office after dark, I ask one of the secretaries to escort me to the parking lot.

The letters accused me of being "disgusting, ignorant, offensive, bigoted, pompous, crude, and insensitive," thus furnishing my wife the opening to ask, "Are you sure those women have never met you?" The tone, emotional fervor, and unremitting literalness of their replies conjured up visions as frightening as the Harpies in Greek mythology and constituted what might be considered by some as compelling evidence on the subject of which group has the least sense of humor. However, to avoid another spate of vituperative letters, I have decided to postpone indefinitely the announcement of my decision. I certainly don't want to risk saying anything that would be taken by the militant feminists as patronizing. After all, some of my best friends are women. Why, I was raised by one.

(18 March 1980)

Send In
the Clowns

Television commentators, newspaper editorialists and professional hand-wringers throughout the country are forever decrying voter apathy in the United States and wondering aloud as to why our well-educated and prosperous electorate persistently manages to stay away from presidential elections in droves.

As the current presidential elections near, growing numbers of distressed and concerned citizens (most of them, I admit, bored housewives or neighborhood children working on civics projects) seek me out and inquire into the cause of this calamity. My answer is simple but it inevitably staggers them with its irrefutable insight: "Televised Nominating Conventions."

How can we reasonably expect the American voters to take seriously any candidate served up by a crowd which looks like something that would result if you crossed a Shrine convention with the studio audience from "Let's Make a Deal."

I offer in evidence the recently concluded looniness in Detroit called the Republican National Convention where several hundred middle-class Americans dressed in cowboy hats, Indian headdresses, straw boaters, pith helmets, and

assorted novelty store paraphernalia, spent four highly public-
ized days blowing air horns, popping balloons, walking on
stilts, and cheering banalities; and ultimately nominated for
the presidency a geriatric marvel who appears to have
extended his life span by periodically soaking himself in an
elixir consisting of equal parts Grecian Formula 44 and Wild
Root Cream Oil, and who, if in politics at all, should logically
be running for mayor of St. Petersburg. (As one disrespectful
Democrat observed, "The guy's hair may be black but his face
is falling so fast his make-up man has to wear a hardhat.")

From the opening ceremony it was destined to be a comic
and bumbling enterprise. Party officials presented Gerald
Ford with a "solid gold" medallion and he promptly fumbled
it, giving credence to a story in the *National Enquirer* quoting
a well-known psychic who believes that Ford is possessed by
the spirit of Chevy Chase. The burlesque continued with the
vice-presidential selection. Here Reagan's Hollywood experience proved invaluable and the Ford chase scene had all the
timing, taste, and merriment of "The Three Stooges in
MoTown."

One of the most unsettling aspects of the extravaganza was
the contrast between the "Looney Tunes" and "Merry Mel-
ody" doings on the convention floor and the somber pontifical
air in the TV news booths. I think it would be better for
consistency's sake if during these conventions Walter Cronkite
wore a fake nose and mouse ears, and David Brinkley and
John Chancellor would occasionally do some vaudeville
blackouts and pummel each other with goat bladders.

This is not to say that the proceedings were completely
without dignity. The entire country was hushed and over-
whelmed with the majesty of the moment when the orchestra-
tors of the convention brought out, get this . . . Donny and

Marie Osmond! It makes you wonder if Jane Wyman is voting Republican.

I'm not saying that we should do away with nominating conventions. Everyone has a deep-seated need to act silly and make a fool of himself from time to time . . . that's why alcoholic beverages and television game shows were invented. I'm just suggesting that they be kept secret from the American public lest there be generated in the ranks of the voters an overwhelming appetite for military juntas.

The real question is, will the upcoming Democratic doings inspire the American voters with the seriousness and high purpose of the election process? I think the prospect for improvement is pretty bleak. If the party of the rich, privileged, and upper middle-class staged a convention that looked like a combination between an old-fashioned tacky party and "Saturday Night Live," what can we hope for from the party of Jefferson, Jackson, and Billy Carter?

The poor Democrats have yet to convince Kennedy that the primaries are over and he keeps darting about like a Japanese holdout on Okinawa making shrill and unintelligible pronouncements about what he'll do when he is president. While all of this is going on, former conservative Republican John Anderson (you remember him; he's the guy with Ronald Reagan's hair) is Bull Moosing around the world trying to upstage everybody. My guess is that the funny hat factories are working around the clock and if the Democratic convention is anything like the Republican effort, I wouldn't be surprised if they wound up nominating Milton Berle.

Detroit's convention motto was "Detroit Loves a Good Party"; maybe New York ought to consider "Send in the Clowns."

(25 July 1980)

Gone with the Wind

My continuing quest for the cause of the precipitous decline in learning skills among American teenagers is well known. The incisive and articulate thesis of mine attributing it to brain damage from attending rock concerts was first published in these pages and has since been the subject of countless seminars, scholarly papers, and academic journals throughout the land. Savants from centers of scientific inquiry as far away as Austell, Villa Rica, and East Marietta have mentioned the Nobel Prize and there has even been some talk that I might be invited to speak to a Rotary Club. (Such praise is, I believe, excessive. However, I do maintain a current passport and a brief but gloomy speech on government interference with the free enterprise system should Stockholm or a Rotarian choose to call.)

For some time following the publication of my exposition it was thought that my analysis was dispositive of the question. Pasteur, they said, had uncovered the cause of spoilt milk; Lister had discovered the germ (thus paving the way to the processing of Listerine which enabled countless advertising executives and stockbrokers to return to their offices after lunch and saved more marriages than family counseling); and Steed, well, Steed had rooted out the cause of teenage mental numbness.

However, complacency in the scientific community was short-lived and soon shattered when questions began to surface as to whether rock concerts were the only cause of this growing affliction. Many parents who were convinced that their oily-pored offspring had never attended a rock concert, would come to my chambers to plaintively urge: "There must be other causes as well. My Jeffrey (or 'Mark,' 'Jennifer,' 'Scott,' to name just a few of the monickers in current middle-class vogue or, in the working classes, 'Debbie,' 'Tammy,' 'Wanda,' or 'Roy') . . . has never been within five miles of a Blue Oyster (or Doobie Brothers, Electric Light Orchestra or Meatloaf) concert but he begins his sentences with 'like,' uses 'go' as a transitive verb in place of 'say' (as in 'She goes, "Have you had an acne transplant?" and I go, "What?" '), punctuates every declarative sentence with a 'ya no' and thinks that Mork is the television character whose vocabulary is most worthy of emulating."

Well, nothing touches my heartstrings more than a distraught parent (particularly those comely mothers in the thirty-five to forty-year-old range) and I immediately determined to restudy the question by observing clinical material available in my own household in the persons of my three teenage children.

Theory after theory was tried and abandoned and finally, just as I was about to give up the study and admit failure, the answer flashed into my mind with stunning clarity—Electric Hairdryers!

I remembered vividly some years back, when my oldest child was barely in his teens, being abruptly awakened by a noise which convinced me that he was trying to cut up his bathtub with a chainsaw or that he had successfully stuffed one of his sisters in the Cuisinart. It was, of course, as all parents of teens have guessed, nothing more than my teenager leaning into his gale-force blow dryer.

In time his sisters took up the practice and our mornings began to sound like a C-5A being tested at Lockheed. My suggestions to them that, given time, their hair, like mine, would dry on its own without mechanical intervention, were met with looks the patient give those who are obviously crazy but probably not dangerous. In time my wife and I learned to lip read and pantomime and the whine of the hairdryers became routine to everyone except our dog who still gets in the car and tries to roll up the windows.

The answer, then, for those parents who aver that their children have never attended a rock concert but whose PSAT scores barely moved the needle, is hairdryers. Their brains, having been fricasseed daily throughout their teenage years, now resemble overbaked apples. I am pleased to share with mankind my firm prediction that if crewcuts and Montovani ever come back in style, SAT scores will inevitably soar.

In the unlikely event that there are teenagers who have neither attended rock concerts nor used blow dryers but who still appear to have the IQ of Chuck Barris, I am always available for parent conferences—particularly with those thirty-five to forty-year-old mothers.

(13 August 1980)

Obese Abuse (or, Fat People Need Love Too)

With all this talk about battered women, I'd like to know if anyone is interested in or trying to prevent an equally serious and even more widespread problem—obese abuse. While I certainly agree that it is reprehensible for any husband to roll his wife in eggs, milk, and bread crumbs, I feel just as strongly that there is a need for increased concern and perhaps even legislative action in the area of caustic remarks by wives (or husbands) regarding weight control problems of their spouses.

At a recent cocktail gathering, an unknown but very comely lady approached me and said, "You remind me of Erma Bombeck a little." Before I could respond my wife replied, "If you saw him in a bathing suit he'd remind you of her a lot." This, I submit, is the kind of loutish and insensitive remark one might expect from someone who feels "stuffed" after a half piece of toast.

I will concede that Erma and I are both what Jane Russell calls "full-figured" but still, despite my previously acknowledged tendency to "bunch up" when sitting down, we are, I think, most pleasant in appearance.

I have long since made a separate peace with my weight problem by coming to the mature judgment that if you can't be effective you can at least be philosophic. I thought it a significant breakthrough when at age forty I made a firm resolution to no longer continuously hold my breath on the beach. A second breakthrough was my decision to quit reading the myriad diets that appear so relentlessly in every magazine from *Redbook* to *Dragstrip Journal*. After forty years I finally realized they were all fads, mostly ridiculous and completely ineffective, and that you could go blindfolded to any magazine counter and pick up something along the following lines:

1. The All-You-Can-Eat Diets—These permit you to eat all you want provided you limit your selection to squash and guavas.

2. Dr. Stillman's Water Diet—Completely ineffective and produces a noticeably bad side effect— "audible sloshing."

3. Dr. Hosea Williams's Driving School and Weight Control Clinic—Just another "crash" diet.

4. The Orson Welles/Paul Masson Diet—You can trust Paul to sell no wine before its time but it would be a grave error in judgment to leave Orson alone for even a moment with your groceries.

5. The Eat-Only-When-Standing-Up Diet— This breakthrough promised that you would "startle your friends" with rapid weight loss. I tried the diet for a week and the only person I startled was the maître d' at Nikolai's Roof.

I've also found that if one follows a few commonsense rules there will be less preoccupation with a weight problem. For example, an overweight person is much less conspicuous while

wearing a bathrobe except, of course, at wedding receptions, business lunches, etc. In addition, one should avoid buying clothes at trendy shops like Britches which, if they carry your size at all, characterize it as the "Porker" or "Chubbette" model. Instead, trade with establishments which euphemistically term suits shaped like Hefty Bags as their "Executive Cut."

I would also caution against weighing on any scales in a doctor's office. They are always high. My surly spouse (have you ever noticed that thin people are rarely jolly?) suggested that my scales might be as high as those in the doctor's office if I ever let go of the towel rack while weighing. I thought it just as well not to let her know that the last time I tried that maneuver the digital readout on my scales flashed "One At A Time Please."

In summary, my advice is not to worry about weight control unless there is clear and present danger of terminal obesity. In that connection I have prepared and am willing to share "Dr. Steed's Seven Danger Signals for Terminal Obesity." They are:

1. Being ordered off a public beach for having no top to bathing suit.

2. Chrome on refrigerator handle shows noticeable wear.

3. Dirt accumulates in rings around neck during summer months.

4. Angle of necktie exceeds forty five degrees beyond vertical.

5. Hallucinations about being followed by the chicken in "Smilin' Jack."

6. Wife needs seat belt or Velcro fasteners on

sheets and pajamas to keep from rolling to your side of bed.

7. Sudden disappearance of feet.

Unless at least four of the seven signals appear, thin spouses should be required to keep their own counsel and their more ample mates should strive to maintain a sense of humor about the whole business. My hero in this regard is the beautiful, bubbly, and bountiful opera star, Beverly Sills, who, having agreed to make a Western movie, insisted on a clause in her contract to the effect that if the script called for her to ride off into the sunset, the producers were required to find a horse whose behind was bigger than hers. I'd ride off with Erma or Beverly. Anytime.

(17 November 1980)

Dr. Jones
Draws the Line

Enough, as they say, is enough. I have stood by silently while various "sophisticated" columnists, letter writers, public officials, and even editors (they of little faith, acid pen, and curled lip) have pummeled and pilloried Dr. Bob Jones III, president of the eponymous institution of enlightenment in Greenville, S.C., for daring to raise his voice in moral judgment against the decadent art at Atlanta's new midfield terminal. The attacks have been vicious and unrelenting.

While the safe and more popular course for me would clearly be to avoid the raging controversy or, worse still, cast my lot with the pack of jackals baying at the good doctor's heels, my conscience demands that I speak out in his behalf.

Lest I be misunderstood, I should hasten to say that in defending Dr. Jones, I do not intend to be drawn into the public clamor regarding the outrageous art at our new airport terminal. The officials in charge of selecting the works displayed there have callously and consistently ignored public taste. Early in the construction phase of the terminal, I wrote them making specific suggestions as to art works that would reflect the level of local enlightenment in art appreciation. My first suggestion, which they rejected out of hand (whatever that means), was a towering reproduction of Gainsborough's "Pinky," dressed, of course, as a Delta stewardess. My second suggestion was that they feature a hanging in the main terminal representing the local art style widely known as "Marietta Modern." Their snippish response was that it would be virtually impossible to find a chenille bedspread that big.

But back to my word in behalf of Dr. Jones. My credentials as counsel for the defendant could hardly be more impressive. They are grounded on overwhelming empathy which springs from what I suspect to be common environments in terms of upbringing and education.

I imagine we both are victims of the sexually repressed and pre-Playboy 1950s (my teenage colleagues and I would cheerfully have killed to lay our hands on back issues of *National Geographic*). We both received our undergraduate training in the cloistered halls of Baptist centers of learning and while my alma mater, Mercer, even then was to Bob Jones University what Harvard is to Massey Business College, the similarities are strong and abundant. One has to have endured such an educational environment to appreciate where Bob Jones, as they say in the newly emerging and staggeringly inarticulate vernacular, "is coming from."

Without ever having set foot on the Bob Jones campus, I can assure you from my Mercer experience that after four years in such an enviroment, a healthy male would be titillated at the sight of dress shields.

In the mid-1950s public nudity was very much an issue at Mercer. Coeds could wear shorts to gym classes but while they were in public view they had to wear a raincoat lest their young bodies excite lascivious thought. (The advantage this gave the Wesleyan students during the bathing suit portion of the Miss Macon Contest was inestimable.)

Stricter still was the rigid prohibition against dancing on campus; any such carnal activity was absolutely proscribed. While editor of the student newspaper, I injected myself into the eye of that theological hurricane by suggesting that contrary to the prevailing view of the Georgia Baptist Convention, modern research indicated that the box step did not cause cancer. I noted further that dancing had been going on at the Wesleyan campus for some time with no noticeable increase in the crime rate in that quarter of the city. For this heretical presumptuousness I found myself once again No. 1 on the prayer list maintained from week to week by the Mercer Ministerial Association and the subject of impromptu "suck-back" sermons by budding Ernest Angleys along the following lines:

> Oh, yes, you fraternity boys, you smoke those filter-tip cigarettes, you go out to Wesleyan College and date those *Methodists*, dance with them, even kiss them—on the mouth—where they *eat*! Well, one of these mornings you're gonna wake up around a big campfire and smell something burning, and *brother*, it's gonna be you!

The point of this autobiographical indulgence is that we should not stand in judgment of Dr. Jones unless we have walked in his shoes. He is not simply speaking out against public displays of nudity. I suspect from my own background that he is genuinely concerned that public nudity will lead to other vices, specifically, mixed dancing. And, as anyone educated at a Baptist college will tell you, it is well known that mixed dancing ultimately leads to that pernicious activity known in the Good Book as "begetting." We've simply got to draw the line somewhere, and Brother Jones opted for an airport Armageddon.

In conclusion, I urge patience and understanding for Dr. Jones. I urge the public officials at the Atlanta airport to turn the other cheek—figuratively, of course, and I urge each gentle reader who supports the good Doctor to send him a word of greeting and encouragement (Dr. Bob Jones III; South Carolina State Home for the Easily Aroused; Greenville, South Carolina 29304) and to send up a prayer for his detractors when turning in at night. In that connection, please remember to get into your Dr. Dentons before doing so; I don't think God hears the prayers of naked people either.

(19 December 1980)

Herr Gütwrench über Alles

Since May 7, 1945, successive generations of American school children have been taught that the United States defeated Germany in World War II. However, in the minds of those hapless Americans who own German automobiles and must deal with the garages that specialize in their care and feeding, the outcome remains very much in doubt.

Having been the owner of a succession of used Mercedes for over fifteen years, I am convinced of the existence of a massive and continuing war effort located in a bunker somewhere in Argentina where malevolent forces continue to develop and implement a long-standing plan to bring America to its knees by means of massive and recurring automobile repair bills.

(There is a similar and equally intriguing rumor, first published, I think, in John Crown's column, that since 1945 the Japanese have planted a quantity of plastic explosives in each small appliance manufactured for export, and that some December 7 in the not too distant future a detonator will be pressed in Tokyo causing our entire country to immediately resemble the less fashionable parts of East Marietta. But that is another story and will be reserved for a subsequent exposé.)

The Robert Ludlums, Ira Levins, and Frederick Forsythes of the world should stop toying with the fanciful *Rhinemann Exchange, Odessa File,* and *Boys From Brazil* fairy tale themes and start looking under the nearest Audis, BMWs, and Porsches for a really sinister plot.

Some might suggest that such paranoia is not uncommon in people with absolutely no mechanical aptitude, who thus are not the best prospects for ownership of sophisticated, high-strung, and finely engineered automobiles. There may be some validity to this position and I am quick to confess to an absolute lack of mechanical aptitude. I can affirm from sad experience that this genuine lack of affinity for things mechanical does in fact put one at a severe disadvantage in negotiating with automobile repairmen.

In one of my early encounters in Mercedes repair matters, the owner of the garage mentioned something about my "overhead valves." Furrowing my brow in an attempt at a knowledgeable look, I asked just how expensive it would be to have the valves relocated to their proper place. The uncontrollable laughter that erupted from under the upraised hoods throughout the shop convinced me that I thereafter would be negotiating under a substantial handicap.

Even conceding an aptitude gap in matters mechanical, I nonetheless persist in my hypothesis that there is something sinister and global in the frequency and magnitude of my repair bills. I think if the FBI would subpoena the records of every automobile repair shop in the country having a name which begins with "Horst's," "Wolfgang's," "Ludwig's," etc., surprising evidence of the hidden front I suggest would soon surface.

My wife, long since exasperated by my theory, asked why I don't simply trade in for a newer model. I explained patiently that in the case of foreign automobiles, as in the case of first wives, experience (and fire-breathing divorce lawyers) has proved that it is far less expensive to make do with the older model. Her well-meant but simpleminded suggestion clearly places her in the ranks of those who have no idea of the prices that new Mercedes now fetch. They are simply beyond the reach of all segments of society other than medical doctors, rock stars, and illegal drug dealers. This, too, I believe, is evidence of the conspiracy.

The "budget-priced" new Mercedes costs in excess of $30,000. The first house I bought cost $12,000 less than that and had two bathrooms and a patio. In that connection, I submit there is evidence that the dark forces of which I speak may well have infiltrated the American automobile industry causing it to produce, to its considerable disadvantage, automobiles of a size capable of accommodating two bathrooms and a patio. Reflect for a moment—you don't see the president of Bavarian Motor Works skulking around Washington with a long face and a tin cup do you?

It may well be that the cash drain has caused my imagination to take a xenophobic turn and that repair shops for German automobiles are not part of the conspiracy I suggest. However, until my investigation is complete, I would offer the following tips to those owners of newly acquired German cars in need of mechanical assitance:

1. Be suspicious of any German mechanic who demands to "see your papers" before agreeing to fix your car.

2. Avoid repair shops where the owner wears a monocle or a Sam Brown belt.

3. Suspect any mechanic who displays a shocked reaction to any reference to World War II or who replies, "Var? Vat Var?"

4. Be extremely wary of assurances that if the engine (clutch, transmission, etc.) is replaced no further repairs will be necessary. That's what they told Chamberlain.

Remember: Today your crankcase; tomorrow the world!

(3 February 1981)

Is There a Doctor in the House?

When the administrators of the two established medical schools in the state heard that Mercer and Morehouse were petitioning the General Assembly for funds to support their own fledgling medical schools, the establishment savants literally (as they say in West Georgia and parts of Alabama) "had a fit and fell in it." The representatives of both of the established and well-heeled schools railed against the alleged need for more medical education and expressed collective outrage that anyone would presume to contest their fervent contention that the community is rushing pell-mell toward a gross overpopulation of doctors. To encourage two more medical schools, they implied, would cause the profession to become so dreadfully crowded that the long-term result would be to throw the practice back into the age of bloodletting and attaching leeches.

The controversy caused me to recall a conversation on the same subject I had with a doctor friend about a year ago. When I proudly informed him that my alma mater, Mercer, had begun a small family-practice oriented medical school, he was literally beside himself (that, incidentally, is his favorite position). "Don't you know," he fulminated, "that the medical profession is already grossly overcrowded?"

His argument was so convincing that a week or so later I resolved to call my dermatologist to attend to a skin blemish I had been neglecting for months. Having heard so much about the doctor deluge, I assumed I would be able to pop by his office after I finished work and I took real pleasure in thinking how happy he would be to stay after his regular hours for the chance of getting a paying patient. I even considered requesting a house call but dismissed it because of the relatively nonacute nature of the malady and the certainty that the dogs in our neighborhood would go beserk at the sight of a horse and buggy.

Imagine my surprise when, after finally getting through a series of recordings and answering services, I reached his appointment secretary who tersely informed me that once the existence and extent of my medical insurance coverage was verified, she would "try to work me in sometime early next fall." Worse yet, when I finally, against all odds, lived to the date of my appointment, I spent half a day in a waiting room which looked like the outdoor field hospital in "Gone With the Wind." I considered informing my fellow sufferers about the surplus of doctors but decided against it after I was unable to determine whether their blotched and angry expressions were the result of dermatological deficiencies or raging anger.

Instead I thumbed through the vintage issues of *Jack and Jill* and *Psychology Today* and reflected on the matter of the pending doctor proliferation, wondering "Where are all these hordes of doctors?" The only evidence I could recall of too many doctors was when I tried to get tee time at the golf club.

Moreover, I thought, if there are too many doctors, why are so many of the practitioners coming into the little towns in rural Georgia from India, Pakistan, Mexico, and Korea? While they are certainly grand and compassionate folks and can probably write a prescription just as illegibly as an American-educated doctor, there is something to be said for a situation where the patient and doctor speak the same language.

The medical profession, I thought, may well be right on the dangers of excess practitioners, and I'm convinced that lawyers could learn a great deal from their brothers in medicine about holding down on the numbers in their professional ranks. Law schools crank out such prodigious numbers of practitioners that chamber of commerce statistics now reveal that in Atlanta alone one person in every three is a lawyer. (Of the remaining two, one is from the ranks of insurance salesmen—many of whom don't even want to sell you a policy but would just like to "drop by and get to know you"—and the third is from the swarm of meteorologists who clog the corridors of our city's television and radio stations. (I predict that in the not too distant future each CB radio purchase will be accompanied by a licensed meteorologist.)

But turning back to the issue of the pending plethora of physicians, I reflected that both sides seemed to have ample but contradictory evidence as to whether we have too many or too few doctors. How then will we know when the number of doctors is really approaching too many? I can't even suggest an answer, but I don't think we ought to worry excessively about it until they start listing their home phone numbers in the telephone book.

(9 March 1981)

The Masters

In the spring a young man's fancy turns to thoughts of love and many an old man's fancy, particularly if he has finished his tax return, turns to thoughts of golf. Setting aside for the moment the intriguing question as to just what a "fancy" is, the approach of the 1981 Masters Golf Tournament would seem to be a good time to peer through the pollen in a serious attempt to get a grip on that metaphysical middle-class passion, the venerable game of golf.

My musings on the subject originally stirred last spring as I sat placidly behind the sixteenth green at Augusta National, which was then under twenty-four-hour attack by azaleas, a gallery approximately the size of Rumania, and the fierce young field of the 1980 Masters.

As I watched the lanky professionals mount their smooth assaults on Augusta's long and lush green fairways and pondered weighty issues such as why the fried chicken breasts were always served without napkins, a matter worthy of deeper reflection came to mind. That thought, which is the subject of this momentous essay, is how the golf which is played at the Masters and the golf which is played by practitioners such as I can logically march under the same banner.

Beginning with the swing itself, one is struck by the contrast between the professionals and the others of us who engage in this royal and ancient pastime. Sam Snead, who in his sixty-eighth year managed to complete last year's Masters in just over par, has a swing so smooth that it seems to be immersed in warm Wesson Oil. By comparison, the swings in my regular foursome (which more or less typifies the thundering herd in which most golfers are included) appear to have been collected from a condemned playground. I was well into my majority before I realized that in golf, as in billards, the result of the stroke is palpably better if at least one foot remains on the ground.

The rapport between a professional golfer and a professional caddie is a wonder to behold. The rapport between a weekend golfer and a weekend caddie can be illustrated by the legendary exchange that took place some years back at one of the city's more prestigious clubs. The golfer, having tacked his way from rough to rough around half the golf course, finally came to a tee shot which required a carry of some 100 yards across a small lake. After dumping five consecutive shots into the water, he waxed philosophic to his caddie, "Golf's a funny game." To which the caddie tersely replied, "It ain't meant to be." A few holes later, having debarked a large segment of woods and finding himself still beyond sight of any fairway, the golfer screamed, "You must be the worst caddie in the world!" "That," said the caddie, "would be too much of a coincidence."

There is even a great difference in dress. The pros are always impeccably turned out—pastel slacks with razor-sharp creases and no back pockets; knit shirts with little alligators, bears, penguins, or other forms of fauna appended, and golf gloves and shoes dyed to match. The duffers, on the other hand, are a sartorial mixed and comically colored bag, and a Saturday morning aerial shot of any putting green in the metro area would look very much like a direct hit on a Shrine parade.

Most striking of all is the decorum and sportsmanship gap that exists between the play of the pros and everyone else. Professionals will go eighteen holes with nothing more than polite exchanges such as "you're away" or "nice shot." My foursome is as long on conversation as it is short on manners and caustic comment comes so frequently that sometimes it approaches the level of infield chatter. While the pros display fastidious sportsmanship, the weekend players—well, just last Sunday when one of our opponents ran in a long and expensive putt and noticed my partner Talley gyrating wildly behind him, he turned and charged, "Admit it! You were hoping I would miss that putt!" "No," Talley replied evenly, "No, I was hoping you would be badly hurt in a serious automobile accident."

As my day at the Masters was about to conclude and my reflections had almost persuaded me that there were no common points of reference between the game played by the pros and the approximation of it attempted by the rest of us, my reverie was interrupted by a dispatch from a companion who had been walking about the course. "Weiskopf," he told me, "just took a thirteen on number twelve! Dumped five straight shots in the water and they're lighting cigarettes on the back of his neck!" "Well," I thought, "there is some common ground after all." And then I remembered the line which Bobby Jones so aptly applied to all who engage in this outdoor masochism. They are all, he said, "dogged victims of inexorable fate." Jones, as usual, hit it right on the button.

(8 April 1981)

Fit to Be Tied
at Nikolai's Roof

I recently received an urgent call from my publishers, Simon & Lipshutz (New York, Philadelphia, and Austell), after they noted the rapidly brewing tempest in the Atlanta newspaper teapot over the disgruntled diner who brought a lawsuit against the management of Nikolai's Roof for being refused service because he was not wearing a necktie. Simon (Lipshutz was busy trying to corner one of the secretaries) said he sensed the possibility of some commercial advantage by further exploitation of this sartorial *cause celebre*, and suggested that I rush into print with a brief preview of a chapter from my upcoming book, *Affectations in Dress and Manner and Other Disgusting Contemporary Trends*. Noting the excessive newspaper coverage already given to this matter, I suggested that we might well be beating a dead horse, but was finally persuaded to proceed after he craftily observed that beating a live one was so unpopular with the Humane Society.

Those readers who are not altogether preoccupied with such mundane news items as American involvement in El

Salvador, President Reagan's breathtaking return to the nine-teenth century and the disquieting *déjà vu* invoked by the presence of troops on the Polish border, may have observed that various columnists in our city's newspapers reacted to the lawsuit against Nikolai's by leaping into the fray and braying at length about the evils of any rule requiring neckties.

In the interest of balanced pretrial publicity, I present herewith my reasoned view on the subject, which, simply stated, is that if Nikolai's prefers that its male diners appear in cravats as opposed to the open-shirt look favored by the gold-chain-and-chest-hair set, savant Steed and the free enter-prise system stand for the proposition that they should have the right to make and enforce their rules. After all, when someone has waited six months for a Nikolai's reservation to ripen and has made the necessary credit arrangements to finance the check, that person is not going to be too thrilled to find a male taxpayer at the next table with an open-front shirt and a chest that looks as though he just coughed up a fur ball. (Some people trace my monomania on this subject to the fact that my glabrous chest resembles, in the words of my devoted wife, "an old man's shin," but even discounting my alleged bias, I think a case can still be made for Nikolai's position.)

In my view, anyone who can afford the prices at Nikolai's can also spring for a tie and, even more important, I think it's high time someone said something nice about the White Rus-sians (I assume it is they and not the Brothers Davis who are running things at Nikolai's). Good lord, the Soviets took away all privately owned land and turned it into communes, mur-dered the Tsar, confiscated the crown jewels and we don't know *where* Anastasia is, but still the relentless persecution continues. Now the carping columnists would deny the des-cendants of the Romanoffs one of their few remaining prerogatives—the right to serve elegant and expensive meals in an atmosphere unafflicted by the sight of chest hair.

My guess is that it is not just the glare of the gold chains and the disgusting abundance of fur below the necks of those gay caballeros which causes elegant restaurants to deny them admittance. Equally odious is the certain knowledge that when you see one of them approaching, you know full well he will be accompanied by a fog of noisome cologne so pungent that one would assume he had just been criminally assaulted by a gang of Avon ladies. Why shouldn't Nikolai's have the right to close their doors to those chain-bedecked and hirsute refugees from singles bars with their pastel polyester suits and wide, pointed, and open collars, and whose Canoe, Brut, Macho-Musk, etc., can do permanent damage to the olfactory nerves of other diners at a distance of twenty paces? The last time my wife let me go to Harrison's alone, I had to fight my way through a cloud of effluvia consisting of industrial strength Aramis so strong that when I finally made it to the bar, I asked for a respirator instead of a drink. If one of those Peachtree John Travoltas by happy chance were to wander into the uncharted regions of the North Georgia mountains wearing a gold necklace and smelling like the Gabor sisters, he might well find himself an unwilling participant in a reenactment of the love scene from "Deliverance."

I say stick with it to Nikolai's, and I offer a final and friendly piece of advice to the open-shirted diner who brought suit against them. When you show up in court you'd better be wearing a four-in-hand; the judges all do, and some of them can be even crankier than a maître d'.

(30 April 1981)

Naked to
Mine Enemies

Celebrity roasts, like demolition derbies, TV game shows, and mud wrestling, are a uniquely American invention. Why any gentle, sensitive person would submit himself to appear before a crowd of bloodthirsty spectators and be verbally flayed by alleged friends is an interesting question. Several Friday evenings past, the question suddenly became less academic and significantly more urgent as I came momentarily out of a daze to find myself the victim of such an atrocity.

It was staged by my alma mater, Mercer University, in the Macon City Auditorium before a crowd of 600 or 700 perverse revelers who looked as though they would have paid to see a root canal. (Perhaps, before proceeding, it would be well to furnish an aside as to how this shy and retiring citizen was thought by the sponsors of such an event to be sufficiently notorious for the honor. The simple fact is that Mercer is so small and its alumni so undistinguished that any who own a tuxedo outright and whose picture has appeared in an Atlanta newspaper are thought by the innocents at the university to have achieved celebrity status. With the field thus narrowed and the other eligible candidates showing more nimbleness, I somehow got the nod.)

It was a long experience which was, at the same time, exhilarating and numbing. Well into the evening, someone leaned over and asked me "How are you enjoying the roast?" That immediately brought to mind another famous question asked under similar circumstances, namely, "Aside from that, Mrs. Lincoln, how did you like the play?"

With the former Macon mayor, Buckner Melton, as the allegedly impartial master of ceremonies, I was successively assailed by Griffin B. Bell, Ruth West Garrett, Hal Gulliver, Martelle Layfield Jr., and Jack H. Watson.

Editor Gulliver, not content with having fed on the carcass overly long at the roast, sought to drag the happy memory of the experience back to his lair for further gnawing. This resulted in a column on the event in which I was further pilloried. With his flat learning curve, notoriously short attention span, and native South Georgia torpor, I was amazed he remembered the evening so vividly.

Some suggested that he may have been piqued by my response to his portion of the roast. Gulliver, awash in brilliantine, appeared in an ill-fitting rented tuxedo, waving one of his ever present Hava-Cheapos (I have tried to convince him that cigars of that quality are manufactured primarily as breath fresheners for people who eat dead birds) and performed very creditably with some vicious japes which drew considerable laughter and applause.

I, on the other hand, followed my standard rule which is that a soft answer turneth away wrath (I don't know why it is, but anytime I get within three miles of the main Mercer campus I start sounding like Ernest Angley), and replied to his

73

invective with the following mild sally:

> What can I say about that artful roaster, the Lowndes County Laureate—Hal Gulliver? Actually, I prepared no response to the anticipated remarks of Gulliver because all of my life I have lived by the adage that you should never get in a battle of wits with an unarmed man. How was I to know that he would get his publisher Jack Tarver to write his material? The reason I know Gulliver didn't write it is because every sentence had a noun and a verb.
>
> I once asked Jack Tarver how he happened to choose Gulliver as editor of the *Constitution*, and his answer, like all Tarver statements, was wonderfully straightforward. He said, "The others wanted to get paid." Many readers of Gulliver's hard-hitting column have suggested that he really ought to be writing for the *Journal* rather than the *Constitution*. The reason, of course, is that people reading an evening newspaper have less reason to complain when they are put to sleep.

The other roasters were as gleefully rude as Gulliver but, lacking a newspaper column, had to content themselves with a single time at bat. Judge Bell declared with conviction that "Steed has written far more than he has read." Ruth Garrett observed that my confidence in myself was a wonderful thing to behold in a time when so many people believe in no god at all. Jack Watson, after declaring that my tuxedo was made by Supp-hose, went on to say that my physique had been a winner in many events . . . "most of them wet T-shirt competitions." Layfield's portion of the roast must have been hilarious but he giggled so much during its delivery that it was incomprehensible to everyone else.

The whole experience made me think for the moment that someone had prepared a table for me in the presence of mine enemies, but, on more sober reflection, I determined that I probably more nearly fit Oscar Wilde's famous description of George Bernard Shaw: "Oh no, he is not important enough to have any enemies; it is well known, however, that none of his friends like him." Next time I think I'll sign up for the mud wrestling.

(2 July 1981)

Angst for
the Memories

Child psychologists, behavioral consultants, school counselors, talk show hosts, and other trained professionals in matters psychological often attribute adult emotional difficulties to severe embarrassments suffered during childhood.

I suspect there may be some truth in this theorum. I know from bitter experience that being put on a Greyhound Bus as a college-bound boy from Bowdon, with nothing more than a shoe box of fried chicken, a rubber sheet, and a lapel sign reading "Put this boy off at Mercer" did precious little for my self-image. As a historical aside, I still remember that as I was boarding the bus my father put his rough hand on my shoulder and gave me the only words of advice he ever offered. He said "Son, try to get a seat by the window and when you get to school don't let them make you room with nobody who wears them jockey shorts." Although I never fully comprehended the exact meaning of his counsel, it is a code I've always tried to live by.

While the psychological scholars are doubtlessly correct in their assumption about childhood embarrassments resulting in personality or behavioral flaws, I think they give too little study to the fact that adult gaffes can be even more psychologically traumatizing.

I can remember as though it were yesterday a college graduation banquet for members of the Blue Key Honor Society where I, the very epitome of Middle Georgia sophistication, startled the students and professors alike at my table when, in midsentence, I paused to pick up with my fingers and eat a butterball which a waitress had just placed on my bread plate. How someone could have lived twenty-one years and not recognize a butterball I cannot say, but the moment I bit into it there flashed across my brain in marquee-size letters— BUTTERBALL! My effort at recovery by observing to the stunned professor next to me, "Now, that's a good butterball," only added to the general embarrassment.

I was to learn that things didn't get much better in the grown-up world when, after finishing law school and reporting for work at my firm, I was sent to the courthouse to file some papers. The phlegmatic clerk, observing me with my legal papers in hand, asked "Is that a new suit?" to which I replied, "No, I've worn it since college." When word of this reached my firm, the partners in charge determined that I would be better suited to an office practice involving considerably less in the way of public appearances.

Still later, another incident occurred, the memory of which still brings color rushing to my handsome but misshapen face. Having introduced myself on a number of occasions in an apparently slurred fashion, which resulted in the person to whom I was speaking replying, "Hello, Paul," I determined that on the next such opportunity I would be more distinct in pronouncing my name. The chance presented itself at a cocktail party sponsored by the Atlanta Lawyers Club.

As it happened, I was one of two early arrivals, and as I did not know the other lawyer, I straight away gave him a firm handshake with good eye contact and said very precisely, "Hello, I'm Paul Steed." Before he could introduce himself, I tried to recover in a tone which indicated that he had made the mistake and said, "No, that's not right, my name is Bob Steed." By this time it dawned on both of us that I still had a firm grip on his hand, and, as his eyes darted wildly about the room looking for help, I dropped his hand and left purposefully as though on urgent business. Although we were never subsequently re-introduced I am convinced he still recognizes me as I recently encountered him in an elevator and he began to perspire profusely and pretended to be cleaning out his wallet.

I should also point out that if a man's individual capacity to emotionally damage himself through world-class blunders is insufficient, he can increase it geometrically by merely taking a wife. As the poet Ovid once declaimed, "Whom the Gods would destroy, they first get married." (There is some dispute among scholars as to whom the quote should be attributed. with a strong and well-organized minority favoring Mickey Rooney.) In any event, as Premier Trudeau and I can attest, a helpmate can cause just as much damage from embarrassing antics as the principal himself. My most graphic example of this happened in England a couple of years ago, and I haven't been back since.

The unhappy episode began in London in a restaurant, Fortnum and Mason, where my wife and I were dining in the manner typically associated with a long-married couple—that is to say, glum and silent. After various of my attempts at stimulating conversation had provoked no response, I noticed a queer-looking old gentleman with round, steel-rimmed glasses, a mustache, and starched collar come into the restau-

rant and take a seat at the counter. I quietly observed to my wife, who is a great celebrity-watcher, that Rudyard Kipling had just entered the restaurant. To her credit, she gave me a level gaze and said, "Rudyard Kipling is dead." I replied, "I would have thought so but that is he sitting at the counter there." After casing him thoroughly she dived back into her gazpacho with the observation, "He must live around here." I thought she was just returning my legpulling, but several nights later I was dismayed and undone to find that such was not the case.

The distressful evening referred to began with a very elegant dinner party given in our honor by some London friends with a guest list that included several somewhat formal English bankers and their spouses. My wife—who relates in the strongest way to Dorothy Parker's confession that when "talking to English people I always feel as though I have a papoose on my back"—was wonderfully quiet. During the middle of the dinner, however, obviously bolstered by consumption of Scotland's greatest export, she became more voluble. When the hostess asked what restaurants in London we had enjoyed, I answered that Fortnum and Mason was a particular favorite. This harmless reply was followed up by my wife, who observed brightly to the entire company, "And you'll never guess who we saw there—Rudyard Kipling."

During the long quiet period which followed this revelation, I remember wishing that she did, in fact, have a papoose on her back. It would have offered a blessed distraction.

I have no conclusion or solution for all of this, but offer it merely as a subject worthy of thoughtful analysis should some isolated reader be considering abandoning daytime television for a life of sober reflection.

(3 August 1981)

A Day at
the Opera
(Soap)

Anyone who thinks or says that there is no good comedy being written for television these days needs only to have the experience I had recently during a rainy week's vacation at the beach, where I was subjected to hour after hour of the new breed of daytime soap operas. It is absolutely some of the most hilarious material ever to be served up with a straight face.

Four consecutive days of clouds and rain besieged us at our Jekyll Island retreat (we had hoped to go to Sea Island but their screening committee found out about my wife's family). My eighteen-year-old daughter and her thirteen-year-old sister and friend were holding me personally responsible for the inclement weather and the only thing that prevented them from falling on me like the rats in the movie "Willard" was their certain knowledge that if we could stay off each other's throats until after lunch each day, the mindless entertainment of soap operas would numb their febrile brains and stay their hostile impulses.

There is a mind-bending variety of offerings. "Variety," I

suppose, is not the right word because all of them seem to overlap and blend into one another. In fact, the characters are clearly all-purpose and interchangeable. Most of the stars seem barely postpubescent and even the physicians (an all-time favorite soap opera character) look as though they should be playing doctor rather than being doctor.

A universal sub-theme that seems to run through every series is the "mystery pregnancy." Nubile young things are forever turning up in a family way and the balance of the afternoon is given over to inquiring into the paternity of the soon-to-be-sprung offspring. It's almost never the obvious choice. Even the names of the programs suggest this soapy preoccupation with mysterious if not immaculate conception—"All My Children," "The Young and the Restless," and "Ryan's Hope" (included here on the suspicion that Ryan's most fervent hope is that it's not his child). You won't find a more randy and fecund bunch this side of a mink ranch.

Space will not permit a description of all of the programs, but picking one at random should convince a dispassionate observer that all are a mindless mixture of dadaism and theater of the absurd with the social significance of previous television contributions such as "My Mother the Car" and "Gilligan's Island." They appear to be written by the same people who produce the interminable repartee between radio disc jockeys and helicopter traffic observers with, I suspect, an energetic assist from those wordmasters who are responsible for the Shane Diamond Co. commercials.

"General Hospital" (I said they like doctors) is fairly representative of the new breed, and on the episode which I happened to monitor, half of the cast somehow found themselves marooned on a jungle island under the most primitive conditions. Laura, who makes Brooke Shields look matronly, is forced to make do with a polyester sarong but luckily seems to have a cache of makeup somewhere. (She is wearing so much eyeliner that I was convinced she was doing a raccoon impression.) Her hapless suitor, Luke, however, is in such aboriginal straits that before Laura will let him have his way with her she makes him shave with a clam shell.

While he is hopping around, rubbing his face and hooting in pain like Hugh Herbert in an old Pete Smith comedy, they miraculously come upon a jacuzzi bath made out of rocks in the middle of the jungle. She coyly says she will bathe if he promises not to look and, in the middle of daytime TV's titillating jungle recreation of Hedy Lamar's momentous scene in "Ecstasy," their friends Robert and Tiffany just happen to stroll by and stop for a chat. Whereupon they all launch into dialogue so wildly improbable and incredibly banal that it beggars description.

If something as mundane as a job or a weak stomach is keeping you away from this extraordinary form of entertainment, you can get the same giddy effect from snorting a line or two of *Comet* and reading the summaries of each of the programs which appear every Saturday in the Weekend Magazine. Witness the following verbatim and unedited sampling from last week:

> *General Hospital.* Rose and Hutch are falling for one another. Disguised as a hospital orderly, a hit man plants a bomb in Hutch's hospital room. The house of Cassadine is an underground palace on a deserted island. The Cassadines' oldest brother Meko demonstrates a chilling underground device which if unleashed could control the world. Luke, Laura, and Scorpio feel the effects of the energy-producer when they suddenly turn cold on the tropi-

cal island. Tiffany runs across Scorpio but promises to keep his secret. Bobbi asks Noah's wealthy uncle to help her find Luke. Gail is told by Monica that Susan is expecting Alan's child. Ann fears she is losing Jeff. Heather tells her mother she didn't kill Diana and pleads for Mrs. Grant's help. Sara gives Joe a papier mâché object shaped like a gun.

Newton Minow, you were almost right, but as far as the new daytime soap operas are concerned, television is a "half-vast wasteland" which should appeal to only those viewers whose brains are obviously receiving a severely curtailed supply of oxygen. I'm having both my daughters checked as soon as we can get an appointment.

(21 October 1981)

Nuclear Calm

When Army Major General Robert Schweitzer, the top military officer on the National Security Council, made a speech recently to the effect that the Soviet Union was "on the move" and predicted that the Red Menace was "going to strike," the Reagan administration caused him to be removed from his post in a manner very much like a mailbag leaving a rail siding.

I think the general got a bum rap. If thirty years of low pay, shining his shoes every day, and having to dress like a doorman at the Ramada Inn doesn't entitle a major general to do a little sabre rattling in an effort to hone the hackles of his troops, the whole system ought to be reworked.

Surely the Reagan administration, so often in step with the Moral Majority, appreciates the eternal biblical verity of the shibboleth that "there will always be wars and rumors of wars." My guess is that the general was just trying to put a little punch in his relentless schedule of speaking engagements and thought that the certain promise of nuclear holocaust might

pique the interest of some glassy-eyed Rotarians who thereto-
fore had been picking at their chicken and pondering the
merits of the "Four Way Test."

Perhaps I tend to be too philosophical about the ever-
pending prospect of Armageddon, but growing up in World
War II and its atomic aftermath inevitably resulted in a philosophy for me not unlike the alternate title to "Dr. Strange-
love," namely, "How I Learned to Stop Worrying and Love
the Bomb."

In fact, the whole subject evoked gentle waves of nostalgia
in this regard and my thoughts were turned to Bowdon, Georgia, in the early 1950s where teenage philosophers of the
Atomic Age solemnly debated the morality of locking good
friends out of their bomb shelter. We were convinced at the
time that Bowdon was a prime military target for the Soviets
because it was the site of a titan in the military-industrial
complex—the Bowdon Rubber Company. The fact that the
company only produced bicycle handlebar grips never weak-
ened our conviction that we would be among the First To Go.

Even before the mushroom-cloud days, I was growing
accustomed to the threat of extinction by military action. In
1938, at the age of two, I arrived in Savannah with my family
who had fled our West Georgia home because of religious
persecution. (My people were members of a small cult on the
Georgia side of the Alabama line called the Vichyssoise Baptists. They believed that true salvation could only be obtained
by rigorous fasting, hip baths, and washing each other's feet in
cold potato soup.)

I still have very vivid memories of wartime paranoia in
Savannah; and perhaps my most vivid in that respect is of the
evenings when my father and his friend, Lee Cook, would let
me go with them to the top of the old Liberty National Bank

Building where, as air-raid wardens, they would keep their high-powered binoculars faithfully trained on the nearby Manger Hotel. Even though I was only six or seven years old, I remember thinking a bit uneasily that if the Germans decided to attack Savannah they probably wouldn't come through the Manger Hotel.

When I suggested to my old man many years later that he and Lee Cook may not have been the most effective Allied forces against the Axis onslaught, he just kept watching television and said, "They never bombed Savannah did they?"

My point is that if we aren't used to living under this nuclear cloud by now, we ought to be, and President Reagan ought to let General Schweitzer go back to making his speeches. I'll bet they make those Rotarians sit up straight.

(6 November 1981)

Secrets to Conjugal Bliss

Often, in the sea of clamoring clients customarily gathered in my outer chambers, there will appear the face of a young friend seeking advice of a more personal nature. With the thoughtfulness and magnanimity which typically characterizes great men of all callings, I will abandon more weighty pursuits to take the youngster aside and counsel him on his personal difficulties.

Just such an opportunity arose recently when Capers, a newlywed of some few weeks, tugged at my sleeve (and, I must say, at my heartstrings), and beseeched me to share with him a few nuggets from my well-known treasure-trove of advice on marital relations.

Obviously, word had spread of my new book, which, though still in the galleys, promises to be a veritable road map to marital bliss. It has been characterized by my publishers, Simon & Lipshutz (New York, Philadelphia, and Austell), as being a work of such overwhelming sensitivity that even Phil Donahue and Alan Alda will twitch in unrestrained envy on reading it. Entitled *Locked Twenty-Three Years in an Unhappy Marriage* or *Wives Are People, Too,* it is a simple, straightforward account filled with my own personal tips for achieving and maintaining marital nirvana. There is already some talk of a movie and Lipshutz recently scurried to the coast to, as he put it, "hammer out a deal." While such thoughts are premature, I have given some preliminary consideration to casting, and I see Robert Redford playing me while the role of my wife would likely go to Zazu Pitts or Charles Bronson.

Sensing that in sharing with young Capers a few kernels from the silo of wisdom represented by the book, I would be making a good investment in a long and happy marriage, I proceeded to do just that. His eyes widened in obvious amazement and admiration as I set forth just a few lucid principles which were, at the same time, simple yet profound. In the hope of producing the same effect on an admiring and needy public (and, in the process, hyping the sale of the book), I have resolved to noise abroad a limited sampling of the book's collected wisdom at this time.

One of the first and most obvious areas where extreme connubial caution should be practiced by husbands is dealing with the well-known and scientific fact that women have a decidedly accelerated aging process. For example, while I am still attractive and maintain a youthful appearance, my wife, who is only twelve days older, is often mistaken for the Queen Mother of Bulgaria. Many years spent in rigorous sunbathing and scowling at me and the children have caused her face to reach that delicate stage of deterioration when it would seem prudent to switch from makeup to Neetsfoot Oil.

My advice is that husbands avoid any mention of this unhappy biological phenomenon, even in a light or jocund vein. When I humorously brought up the subject of a face-lift with my spouse, and jokingly suggested in the presence of some of our friends that it would not only improve her looks but from the excess skin we would likely have enough for a small overnight bag and a pair of moccasins for each of the children, she vented her spleen by trying to remove mine with a nearby spatula. The woman has virtually no sense of humor.

Another extremely sensitive area is that of personal grooming. If you are going out for an evening with your wife and the outfit she turns up in doesn't suit you, never (a) laugh uncontrollably, (b) say "Are you going to wear *that*?" or (c) make mention of a costume party or a Shrine parade.

My wife's bizarre leanings in matters of dress once caused my friend Allison to ascribe to her an extraordinary talent for finding out what was going to be ugly in upcoming fashions and wearing it a year ahead of anyone else. When I passed along his comment to her and offered to administer the public caning he so richly deserved, she simply went into a towering rage—at me. (In the movie, the part of Allison will be played by Marty Feldman.) In this same general area, I have learned that it is best not to point out that a wife's hose are baggy unless you are absolutely sure that she is wearing hose.

The book also seeks to dispel a good many myths which have grown over the years in the area of marital relations. For example, whoever came up with the idea that "honesty is the best policy" obviously never gave a straight answer to a wife who asked, "How do you like my hair?" One should also disregard the old saw to the effect that couples should never go to bed angry. It sounds good in theory, but in practice it would result in staying up all night about three times a week.

The book contains an entire chapter which can be encapsuled in one word—LISTEN. A favorite tactic of wives the world over is to wait until a husband is sufficiently into the newspaper or television so as to achieve a trance-like state, and then spring some important question or disclosure. Failure to listen carefully has caused me to (1) buy a dog, (2) agree to a trip to Europe which I couldn't afford, and (3) join the Methodist church.

I could go on, but then you might not buy the book or see the movie. Suffice it to say that Gloria Steinem, who read it with tear-glistened eyes, said, "If all husbands were this sensitive there would be no need for the ERA."

I couldn't agree more. As I have always said, "There's no such thing as a feminist wife; there are only insensitive husbands."

(4 December 1981)

A Night at the Opera (Vienna)

A few weeks back I found myself sitting in a gilded box at the Viennese Opera with a severe dark woman later identified as my first wife. Taking into account the fact that the full spectrum of her musical interests ranges only from Ernest Tubb at one end to Rosemary Clooney at the other, one might reasonably wonder why we were attending the opera. And, taking into account that she had never ventured beyond Carroll County's borders until the Bowdon High School senior class made its legendary trip to Washington, D.C., in 1954, and that her most fervent travel goal for many years thereafter was someday to "see Rock City," one might reasonably ponder what the two of us were doing in a spot so remote and exotic as Vienna.

As to the last question, considerations of national security preclude complete candor on my part, but it is widely known that certain trustworthy former second lieutenants have, from time to time, been pressed into secret and sensitive international service in their country's behalf. There, I have probably said too much as it is. In any case, I had been moving stealthily about the streets of Vienna with a turned-up collar and looking, I ventured, very much like an early Joseph Cotton in "The Third Man." My wife agreed about the "Third Man" look, but suggested that instead of "early Joseph Cotton," I looked more like "late Orson Welles."

As to the opera, I can only say that it was a slow night on Austrian television, which doesn't even come on until 7:00 p.m., and on which everyone, women included, looks like TV-5's Dale Clark. In all of Austria there are only two channels—bad and worse—and watching it the previous evening had convinced me that "Hee-Haw," if shown in Austria, would win Junior Samples's weight in Emmys.

A fast-talking concierge, sensing my boredom and taking advantage of the language barrier (he spoke English), managed to unload two opera tickets on me and my faithful traveling companion. Before I knew it I was dressed to the nines and sharing a box with a suspicious Austrian couple who bore an unnerving resemblance to Eva Braun and Joseph Goebbels.

The opera itself was very much like the "Gong Show" in German. Thanks to a brief libretto in English, I managed to learn that the plot involved a retired admiral who couldn't stand noise. He was visited by his nephew who had joined a circus troupe and the entire evening was given over to harassing the old man with sustained caterwauling.

For two and one-half hours, he stormed around the stage holding his ears and rolling his eyes while the rest of the company continued to bay, bray, and yodel (not to be confused with the small Viennese law firm by the same name.) By the end of the first act my eyes had glazed over like a sugar doughnut and were rolling in the direction of the exits. But my musically cultured wife (she tap dances and twirls baton) insisted that I stay through the whole enterprise to "build character," pointing out that my only previous opera experience had been when Cab Calloway came to Atlanta in "Porgy and Bess."

When the organized bellowing finally came to an end, Dr. Goebbels screwed in his monocle, turned to me, and inquired in precise English, "You like opera, yes?" Thinking it might be some kind of trick, I replied in an off-hand manner, "In my opinion opera hasn't been the same since Cab Calloway died." I was prepared to expand on my remark with an incisive analogy drawing on Buddy Holly and rock 'n roll, but my wife interrupted with a look so severe that I stopped in midsentence. The Austrian couple, obviously aware that I was onto them, pretended confusion and left quietly without trying to cozen any further information from me.

As we strolled back to the hotel, my wife, noting my peculiar behavior (I kept looking furtively over both shoulders and affected a limp), inquired evenly if I had had too much to drink. "You know," she said, "Cab Calloway isn't dead."

"It's not important," I said with an air of detached mystery.

"Well," she said, "it is to Cab Calloway."

(28 December 1981)

The Time of Your Life

Last Saturday found me in the ten-items-and-under line at the A & P ladened with bananas, cheap red wine, and club soda. (Those who have tried the "Caesar Romero Ten-Day Sangria Diet" will immediately recognize what I was about.) As usual, I found myself behind a hefty matron in a jogging suit with a cart containing thirteen items and a duffel bag full of coupons. I know the General Assembly has a full agenda but it will be absolutely criminal if it doesn't enact legislation this session establishing weight limits for housewives in jogging suits.

While my bananas turned brown (which, many will remember, was the title of an Xavier Cugat hit in the late 1950s) my eyes fell upon a rack containing copies of *The National Enquirer*.

As always, this highly respected publication contained many thoughtful and provocative articles and I browsed through "Jean Dixon Predicts That a Cure Will Soon Be Found for Howard Cosell"; "The Truth About Tip and Tatum

O'Neal"; and "President Reagan's Secret Face-Lifts." (In the Reagan article the *Enquirer* presented no hard evidence to support its premise, but pointed out to the readers that in photographs of the President without his shirt, taken last summer, his navel appeared to be about four inches higher than normal.)

My eyes finally fell upon one of those fascinating articles which permit you to calculate your lifespan. Everyone is familiar with that type of article. You begin with forty years and add or subtract years based on different criteria—"Overweight . . . subtract five years. Exercise regularly . . . add four years,"and so on.

Though the article was interesting and obviously well-researched, it occurred to me during the interminable wait while Our Lady of the Sweatsuit laboriously negotiated her coupon savings, that the criteria used were not altogether complete. There rushed to my mind's eye some obvious omissions:

- Regular medical checkups—add two.
- No prepaid medical insurance—subtract four.
- Rely for medical advice and attention on brother-in-law doctor—subtract five.
- Good credit rating—add two.
- Borrow money from swarthy free-lance bankers whose last names end in vowels—subtract five.
- Sports fan—add three.
- Atlanta sports fan—subtract five.
- Able to vent your emotions easily—add two.
- Have a tendency to vent your emotions to emotional people larger than you—subtract three.
- Become short of breath changing TV channels—subtract five.

- Eat only health food—add zero.

(NOTE: A recent unpublished study has revealed that a lifelong diet of wheat germ, blackstrap molasses, prune yogurt, sunflower seeds, dried guavas, and other health-food staples does not, in fact, extend one's life. The researchers did concede, however, that such a diet makes it seem longer.)

My constructive reverie was interrupted by the sudden appearance of my friend, Talley, who bellowed, "Well, imagine this! In addition to being a lawyer, writer, sportsman, and raconteur, Steed even does his own grocery shopping!"

"Yes," I replied modestly, "I'm a man of many parts."

"Well," hooted Talley in a voice that wilted lettuce three aisles away, "no wonder you get so many laughs when you shower at the Club."

- Friends like Talley—subtract ten.

(28 January 1982)

Make All Checks Payable to 'CASH'

While it is still too early to make any formal announcement, I think it is certainly no secret that many people are urging me to abandon the practice of law and throw myself into the 1982 governor's race. The fact that those doing the urging are predominantly my law partners or clients might give pause to a less public-spirited prospect, but a keen sense of *noblesse oblige* keeps me from giving those factors undue weight.

It is well known that lawyers are particularly susceptible to any suggestion that they possess the unique qualifications for high public office. Even the gentlest breeze bearing such a happy notion further fills their pneumatic egos and warms the cockles of their hearts. (A recent study of the prestigious Emory Clinic revealed that almost ninety percent of all lawyers past the age of forty had heart cockles.)

Moreover, when someone suggests to a lawyer that he consider running for a high elected office, there inevitably stirs in his breast (or loins, depending, of course, on the height of the lawyer) the noble and traditional questions: "What can I do for my country?"; "Why not the best?"; "How can I get a really good government job without having to take the Civil Service Exam?"

It is abundantly clear that I have many obvious advantages over the horde of steadfastly unannounced but frantically campaigning contenders. To name just one, the quiet but forceful dignity of my first name would immediately set me apart from most of the field, whose monikers—"Jack," "Buck," "Billy," "Joe Frank," and "Bo"—sound like they came straight out of a 1935 W.P.A. Manual on "What to Name Your Mule."

Although I don't wish to commit myself to a particular course of action, some of my strategists have suggested that a successful campaign might be waged by simply running against the insensitivity of the current Republican administration—an insensitivity demonstrated by President Reagan's "New Federalism."

While one would have to concede that such a campaign strategy is hardly relevant in a contest to determine who will be moving to West Paces Ferry Road at the end of the year, irrelevant single issues don't seem to stay the hands of other single-issue candidates.

Actually, some of my best friends are Republicans and I am convinced that the New Federalism reflects more of a lack of understanding than a lack of compassion. By way of illustration, when I observed to one Republican friend that the president's proposed cutbacks might prove a hardship, particularly in the area of food stamps, his reply was, "Hardship? What hardship? Who the hell mails food anyhow?"

He then went on to defend the compassionate nature of the Reagan Administration by pointing out that within the last few months the President had ordered the distribution of millions of pounds of government-surplus cheese to the "truly needy." I observed that the magnanimity of the gesture was somewhat diluted when the Republicans sought to take political advantage of it by adopting as their off-year election slogan, "Fondue for you in '82."

The White House also created something of a sensitivity gap in response to questions about the First Family's favorite recipe. The press office originally offered up some exotic crab dish but, after cutback critics pointed out that crabmeat was going for about eleven dollars a pound, the favorite recipe was quickly switched to macaroni and cheese. This nimble menu change provoked a jingle from the ranks of my campaign staff which is sung to the tune of "Yankee Doodle," and goes:

> Ronnie's favorite recipe
> Some critics say it's phony,
> He put some crabmeat on his plate,
> Then called it macaroni.

In addition, as a part of my campaign, I am considering leaking to Jack Anderson the fact that well over ninety percent of the nation's macaroni is grown by rich Republican farmers in southern California.

Leaving the relatively low-priority question of issues aside, it occurred to me that before mounting such a campaign it would be prudent to discuss the prospect with an astute professional. With that in mind, I sought out the *Atlanta Constitution*'s ace political reporter, Frederick "Open Meetings" Allen. The wily journalist is possessed of all the classic attributes of a great reporter: he looks like Clark Kent, walks like Lois Lane, and can cover the General Assembly while keeping a straight face. To say that he was enthusiastic about the prospect of my entering the race would be a gross understatement. His enthusiasm, manifested initially by behavior which most nearly resembled hysterical laughter, was most encouraging. Frankly, I would not be at all surprised to see cautious mention of my name begin to appear in his columns from time to time as someone to watch. While he stopped short of an outright endorsement, he obviously was seeking to encourage me when, after regaining his composure, he confided, "Somebody has to fill the gap left by Roscoe Dean."

Those willing to address envelopes, place a sign in their yard, or curry favor by making early contributions should contact me right away. All checks should be made out to the "Committee Abetting Steed's Hubris," or, for the sake of brevity, "CASH."

(1 March 1982)

Ask Not
for Whom
the Rat Barks

As if good manners were not already in a general and precipitous decline, the telephone company, through the miracle of modern science, has come forth with a new invention which presents its owner with an opportunity to be rude to two people at one time. I am speaking, of course, about the new type of telephone that while its owner is talking to one person, emits an obnoxious sound (somewhat like a rat barking) to alert both parties in the conversation that yet a third party is calling.

Consider the possibilities for just plain bad manners. The owner of the phone must interrupt the current caller, thereby implying (if not stating explicitly) that the happy possibility exists that someone more important is calling. After temporarily slamming the conversational door in the face of the first caller, the owner of the telephone then allows the second caller to interrupt and usually deflates that caller by saying, "I'm sorry, I can't speak to you. I'm talking on another line." (The obvious question that presents itself at that point is, "Well, why the hell did you answer my call if you are talking to someone else?" But apparently this question never occurred to the phone company or to the people who buy this type of device for their phones.) The second party is, at this point, left feeling

    (i) guilty at having been so rude to interrupt, or

    (ii) unworthy and slighted after having been rejected in favor of the original party.

On the other hand, if the second caller sounds more promising than the first, the called party has an excellent opportunity to be doubly rude to the original caller by telling him frankly that something more important has come up.

The biggest market for these devices, according to my informal research, is the "Type A" housewife who simply cannot bear the thought that she might miss one call because she happens to be engaged by another. When I complained to one of them about the discourtesy inherent in the practice, she observed that the owner of the phone did not have to answer the rat bark. However, anyone who has been a party to a call thus interrupted while he is making polite but unimportant conversation will know what I mean when I describe the desperate sense of urgency as the barking noise begins to occur. Respiration quickens; the heartbeat increases; and the original caller senses an overwhelming need to say something significant so as to justify the continued courtesy extended in being allowed to stay on the line.

When measured against the urgent possibility that the incoming call is likely bringing news of the death or mangling of a loved one, the receipt of a large government grant, or a report that the rabbit died, every word uttered by the original caller begins to seem incredibly tedious, insignificant, and banal.

This new and obnoxious device clearly eclipses two long-standing pet peeves of mine in the pantheon of rude telephone behavior. The old-fashioned telephone discourtesies of which I speak are, first, those fostered by dreadfully progressive parents who not only permit, but encourage their tiny tots to answer the telephone and bait helpless adults to a white lather by either speaking in a Gerber-gurgling gibberish or engaging in Captain Kangaroo patter ("Who is this?"; "Can *you* tie *your* shoes?," etc.) which ultimately has the caller sobbing for adult intervention.

The second traditional type of intolerable behavior is that of the mother who conducts a stereophonic phone conversation with the caller on one channel and underfoot children on the other. So many of what I hope will be intelligent telephone conversations are forever being interrupted by exclamations such as "Don't eat that in here!"; "Mr. Hamster doesn't like to be in the food blender"; "Little Norman, don't put that in your sister's nose!" (And, while we are on the subject, I think the General Assembly should pass a law prohibiting parents from giving children their own first names and then calling them "Little" Lamar, "Little" Roscoe, etc., for the balance of their natural lives. Such legislation would, in my judgment, significantly reduce the current volume of axe murders of parents by festering, fully grown teenagers who have been thus stigmatized.)

The new device of which I complain transcends such old-fashioned boorishness and represents a clear triumph of technology over common sense. I suppose we should just be thankful that it was so long in being invented. Imagine the consequences had it been an original feature of the telephone:

"Mr. Watson, come here, I need . . . "

"Hold it Alex, I've got another call coming in."

We might still be communicating with drums.

(11 March 1982)

Designing
for Dollars

If there's an all-time honor roll of self-serving quotations, high on the list will be the following philosophical gem I read a few days ago in the supersleek Fifth Avenue quarters of those golden purveyors of status—Gucci: "Quality is remembered long after price is forgotten. Aldo Gucci—1938."

What a wonderful bit of philosophy for a shopkeeper. It ranks right along with a remarkably supportive deep thought once uttered by a sage very close to me: "If you like it, buy it. Mrs. Robert L. Steed—1963."

As I tracked through midtown Manhattan, following my determined wife who, with only a handful of credit cards and a quiet, grim resolve, can do more for a local economy than several small federal programs, I reflected anew on the extraordinarily low gullibility threshold that Americans have for the sale of status in general and designer labels in particular.

Our first stop in Gotham City was to purchase a pocket-book of a particular brand—Bottega Veneta—which, I believe, is being marketed in the United States by Italy as a retaliatory measure for World War II. My wife explained patiently that the "relatively high" cost of the exclusive line was a function of workmanship and material. Looking at the price tags convinced me the bags must have been made from the gums of a live tiger.

I was next subjected to the haute couture of a new designer, Kamali, I think, though that does sound more like an entree at Taco Bell than a rising star in the fashion galaxy. Ms. Kamali has managed to make a fortune by peddling belts and headbands with sweatsuits and serving up the result for more than it used to cost to outfit a family of four at the Belk-Rhodes store in Carrollton.

When I tried to suggest to my wife that we might have saved money by buying the belt, headband, and sweatsuits separately at Oshman's, she gave me a gaze so baleful that it foretold without words the keen possibility of a prolonged suspension of conjugal bliss. (I have long since learned that one should never try to pet a dog when it is eating or reason with a wife when she is shopping.)

A day on Fifth Avenue would convince even the most casual observer that on the matter of paying expensive prices for anything with a designer label, the American buying public has become completely unhinged. Grown people in New York were lining up to pay good money for luggage, briefcases, and handbags with a Louis Vuitton label which, if my eyes didn't deceive me, were fashioned from one hundred percent genuine handcrafted plastic. That's right, plastic. If Monsieur Vuitton can persuade the American public to pay staggering sums for plastic bags with his initials on them, I believe there is a good chance we can revive the flagging industrial situation in North Georgia by getting Yves Saint Laurent to bring out a line of designer chenille bedspreads.

Not content with the clothing scam, the fashion designers have even gotten into the eyeglass business now and, although the connection between high fashion and optic improvement is a mystery to me, they are stamping their names on spectacles and marking them up for the nearsighted rich. I have a vision of some weakminded myopic putting on his Oscar de la Renta glasses for the first time and exclaiming—as though he had just been gripped by Oral Roberts—"I can see! I can see!" In fairness, I should say that you don't have to go to New York to be aware of this widespread and growing aberration. I'm fully convinced that my fourteen-year-old daughter would buy a live chicken if it were stamped with a small polo player on a horse.

If you detect an anti-designer bias, you are absolutely right. Except for an occasional pair of Orson Welles designer jeans (and I'm more interested in fit than fashion) I have steadfastly refused to participate in the status-label mania that has gripped our country by the throat.

Where will it end? Well, H. L. Mencken, the old Baltimore oracle (not to be confused with baseball team of the same name), said a manly mouthful when he allowed that "Nobody ever went broke underestimating the taste of the American public." It's hard to believe he uttered that prescient sentiment so long before the development of our current madness, which finds us on the very brink of Pucci dental floss, Gucci odor eaters, Ralph Lauren jumper cables and, who knows, Giorgio Armani tombstones. Chic without end. Amen.

(7 May 1982)

I'm O.K., You're O.K.,
But He Smells Funny

In my soon-to-be-published comprehensive study of the contemporary sociological spectrum, a wide band will be devoted to the growing phenomenon of colognes for men.

My publishers, Simon & Lipshutz (New York, Philadelphia, and Austell), are so enthusiastic about this aromatic exposé that they've expressed the possibility that it may well be developed as a property for a made-for-television movie. While they've encountered some legal difficulties with their originally suggested working title, "The Sweet Smell of Success," their zeal for the project remains high. They're already offering the paperback rights under the alternate title (suggested by Lipshutz), "I'm OK, You're OK, But He Smells Funny."

It is, of course, no secret that Ralph Lauren, Halston, Calvin Klein, and others are now heavy into the "male fragrance area." While I have to confess that I've always been more than a little suspicious of any grown man with a full set of teeth who voluntarily chooses to smell like a New York dress

designer, I must concede that the phenomenon has become sufficiently widespread to merit some scholarly literary attention.

In my early postpubescence, the fragrance options were clear-cut and inexpensive: Mennen Skin Bracer, Palmolive After Shave, Aqua Velva, and, for the affluent, Old Spice. These sturdy and serviceable low-powered potions were designed primarily for the therapeutic purpose of healing the layers of epidermis scraped off in the daily process of defoliating one's face. They have now given way to noisome "colognes" with names like Paco Rabanne, Brut (with a pronunciation that has a masculine sound but an aroma that would convince one that the user would likely wear a silk handkerchief up his sleeve and skip a lot), Pour Homme, Eau Savage, and Aramis—all with effluvia strong enough to gag a pulp cooker at a paper mill.

The old "shaving lotions" had two things going for them. They were cheap and, if you didn't like the aroma, you could take comfort in the fact that it wouldn't last long once you hit the open air. Today's blends are so expensive that for the price of four ounces of Pierre Cardin one could have bought enough Aqua Velva to float the Graf Spee. Moreover, the new scents have a half-life equal to that of spent plutonium.

It's bad enough that grown men are walking the streets (and, worse yet, riding the elevators), smelling as though they had just been criminally assaulted by a gang of Avon ladies, but an even more serious and medically related problem has recently surfaced. While I obviously can't let too many cats out of my upcoming literary bag, I will reveal that secret experiments recently conducted by the U. S. Food and Drug Administration have proven conclusively that designer colognes cause terminal gagging in nine out of ten laboratory mice.

(Interestingly enough, the tenth mouse proved totally adaptable to the pungent aromas and began wearing open-front shirts, gold neckchains, and hanging out at Harrison's.)

I close this tantalizing preview of my book with the prediction that the health dangers will have little effect on the frenzied and malodorous state of affairs now consuming the American male. I foresee nothing more than a regulation for separate seating on airplanes or an edict from the U. S. Surgeon General requiring a warning on the labels.

Speaking of labels, if there are any designers out there who have a new scent but are still looking for the right name, I have recently copyrighted a sure-fire possibility. It's short, descriptive and has that wonderfully sophisticated foreign sound— "Ad Nauseam."

(11 June 1982)

Clubs for Women

On the issue of the feminist movement, I have often been unjustly accused of being a raging, insensitive, chauvinist lout. In fact (and in private) I actually have moments so supersensitive and caring in this regard that, if made public, they would cause Phil Donahue and Alan Alda to absolutely twitch in unrestrained envy.

A recent news story tolling the death knell of the Equal Rights Amendment plunged me into such a moment, and my concerned thoughts focused on the problem of what the militant feminists would do now that this monumental ten-year effort had come a cropper.

Of course, there is no end of tremendously important causes to which they might rally. They could join the movement to protect baby seals, but the weather is cold and the work is remote and seasonal. They could join the swelling crowd of voices seeking to free Hosea Williams, though his list of violations is so moving that it would likely require a constitutional amendment to spring him and our automobile repair shops simply can't wait another ten years. Nuclear power is a popular thing to rage against, but the plants, in most cases, are so remote that the shiftless TV camera crews won't even go out to cover a really good protest.

My heart also went out to the husbands of those abruptly causeless militant feminists who are now living in the grip of a terror that their protesting wives might suddenly start protesting around the house. In what channel should this molten energy be redirected? The answer, I think, is clear: mount a nationwide effort to force all male civic clubs to admit female members!

Why should women all over this great nation be denied the privilege of attending weekly luncheon meetings, wearing funny hats, eating rubbery chicken, and listening to a succession of boring speakers, just because of their sex? It's true that many civic clubs have admitted women as "auxiliary" members. The Jaycees have the Jaycettes and, I suppose, the Shriners have the Shrinettes; but that approach seems hollow and empty if the girls aren't taught the password and don't get to know the secret handshake.

The problem, of course, reflects ancient cultural influences and rigidly conditioned biases. Almost every male can remember devoting a good deal of his prepubescent energy to keeping females out of the clubhouse. Even historical figures had solemn opinions on the subject. When George Bernard Shaw was asked if he favored clubs for women, his famous reply was "Only if all other means of persuasion fail."

I frankly think this is a cause whose time has come and urge all those now disoriented and militant mothers to man (excuse the expression) the barricades. I believe an overwhelming majority of the males will join them and march shoulder to shoulder in a unified effort to tear down these insidious barriers. Certainly one of my most painful moments as a father was taking my two daughters aside one evening and, with tears streaming down my ample cheeks, having to tell them that they could never be Rotarians.

And, in closing (increase volume and begin playing "America, the Beautiful" as I obviously warm to my subject), if there are those of you out there who harbor the thought that women might not be equal to the solemn challenge and responsibility of being a Kiwanian, Moose, Odd Fellow, or Lion, just reflect on this bit of wisdom once uttered by a great American philosopher (I think it was either Ralph Waldo Emerson or Truman Capote)—"If you think Fred Astaire was a great dancer, just remember that Ginger Rogers did everything he did—backwards and in high heels."

(25 July 1982)

Turning the Other Chic

In terms of culture and sophistication, my wife of twenty-four years and I are literally light years apart. Though we both were raised in the same small West Georgia town, our opportunities for cultural enrichment were radically different. While, as a youngster, I sat at home listening to our family's splendid selection of Mantovani records and browsing through the legendary Steed library (consisting of an almost complete set of Zane Grey and a handsome collection of Reader's Digest Condensed Novels), my wife-to-be was more likely to be found listening to gospel music on her daddy's truck radio and clipping articles on "Fun Things to do with Okra" from the *Progressive Farmer*.

Thus it is that she is something of a social outcast while I have many society friends and am constantly invited to join the trendy quiche-and-candelabra set for fashionable outdoor concerts at Chastain Park. My wife, who related to Willie Nelson even before he pierced his ears, goes quietly along, but after so many of these super-sophisticated evenings, it is clear from her doleful gaze (and the fact that her nose gets clammy and warm) that she is feeling the call of her country roots and longs to turn the other chic. To humor her and to meet this deep-seated primordial need, I recently organized what I can unqualifiedly recommend as a sure-fire antidote to those who feel they have reached their symphony-and-society gag level at high-toned Atlanta gatherings: a low rent, high gear, laid-back country music cantata at West Georgia's Franklin Music Park.

Last Saturday evening, my law partner, Ruth Garrett, and I promoted the first leg of what is sure to be a momentous cultural exchange, herding a dazed group of mutual friends onto a westbound charter Greyhound for an evening of pure Jerry Lee Lewis in scenic Heard County, Georgia.

To make the transition less shocking to the Chastain-conditioned gourmet set travelling with us, we thought it advisable to include a six-course meal during the bus ride over. Our carefully chosen menu consisted of two Harold's bar-becues, two long-necked beers, a piece of cracklin' cornbread, and a bag of chips.

The Music Park is about two miles south of Franklin on Highway 27 and the locals immediately spotted us as out-of-towners when they saw our bus didn't have a gun rack in the back window.

Any lingering doubts among those in our group that we were up to our ears in counterculture were soon dispelled by the arrival on stage of the "Killer," his radioactive self—Jerry Lee Lewis. With the first few opening notes, he proved he still had his legendary dominance over piano and crowd. Jerry Lee's left hand alone would make Ferrante and Teicher send out for reinforcements. When his right hand comes on board the crowd goes berserk. When he roars into any of his standards—"Great Balls of Fire," "Whole Lot of Shakin'

Goin' On," "Thirty-nine and Holding," "Mama, this Song's for You"—the partisans literally levitate.

At the end of the thoroughly satisfying session, we were as exhausted as old Jerry Lee who, because of recent bouts with tax collectors, ex-wives, doctors and perforated stomachs, is apparently not playing in all the big time spots or making movies like some of the other good ole boys. However, as we filed out of the music hall, our collective sentiments were admirably expressed by a pneumatic, hot-blooded, wide-beamed Heard County debutante who exclaimed, "That Jerry Lee! He's my horse if he don't never win a race!"

If there are those of you within the sound of my voice who are weary of art openings, brunches, outdoor cocktail parties, and Chastain concerts, and who think you've been to the country when you drive through Vinings, try a different slice of life this summer and go visit Hugh Goodson at his Franklin Music Park. There are still some good shows to come. Tell Hugh that Bobby Lee from Bowdon sent you.

(12 August 1982)

That's Easy for You to Say

In 1775, English playwright Richard Sheridan wrote a play called "The Rivals," a character from which gave birth to a word in the English language: "malapropism." The lively Mrs. Malaprop was forever muddling the language and her listeners with skewed renderings of conventional words and phrases such as "They're in for a shrewd awakening."

The redoubtable grammarian, Bergen Evans, contends that a malaprop is worse than a mispronunciation "because a mispronunciation is simply honest ignorance; whereas malapropisms are likely to occur in the speech of those who, ambitious to use fine language but not industrious enough to consult a dictionary, soar above their abilities and display not only their ignorance but their vanity as well."

I heartily disagree with Professor Evans and earnestly contend that malapropisms are a result of faulty hearing, not faulty learning.

Sheridan's famous character, I have long thought, prefigured my wife, who has always been able to convince anyone with whom she is conversing that English is, for her, a second language. I have frequently introduced her into evidence in support of my premise that the malaprop malady is the result of a bad ear rather than a bad brain. The sinewy Mrs. Steed is, for example, an honor graduate of Wesleyan College (she was a classmate of Madame Chiang Kai-shek), reads without moving her lips, can name the capitals of several obscure Western states, and has a growing reputation as an accomplished painter, (it is, however, no secret to art insiders that the *faces* of all of her portraits are actually painted by me). Notwithstanding these tangible evidences of a respectable IQ, she has spawned enough malapropisms to fill a feature-length novel.

The problem, as I suggested earlier, is a bad ear. One simply cannot repeat what one cannot hear. Her shortcomings in this regard are graphically demonstrated any time I attempt to coach her in the pronunciation of any foreign word or phrase. After many trips to Mexico she was determined to learn to order iced tea in Spanish. Though the two words necessary to accomplish this minor feat are simple enough, her first (and last) attempt at this endeavor resulted in the purchase of a gaily colored but rather expensive blanket.

She is at her very best when committing mayhem on a standard cliché with legendary examples such as: "He got them all in one clean swoop" (the logical variation being "one fell sweep"); "He went away in a twit" (evoking images of an angry person leaving in a small pink foreign car); or, in connection with hopeless causes, "You can kiss that one out the window"; or, on the subject of a settled issue, "That, my dear, is a mute question"; or, in the random category, "He was, you know, very well traveled—a voyeur."

Her delivery is so authoritative and convincing that she is seldom challenged. Over the years I have grown to admire her determination in the face of repeated failure and have boasted that when it comes to free-style malapropizing she is without peer.

This claim was recently challenged when I met Bill Steenson of Bethpage, N.Y., who vigorously contended that his business colleague and friend, Tom Cunniffe, deserved to be established as the reigning champ in this area. He offered as evidence a list of Cunniffe sayings which had been collected, authenticated, and catalogued over a period of years.

After examining the list I am compelled to concede his point. It runs six typewritten, double-spaced pages and contains, to give but a few examples, the following: "Just give him a hunchback estimate"; "You can beat a dead horse to death"; "You buttered your bread—now lie in it!"; "He looked him straight in the head"; "You can't put a jewel in a sow's ear"; "We're treading on thin water"; "Mac is breathing down my throat"; "Give me a whole wheat on rye"; "I've got jobs coming out of my gazebo"; "He came running in on bended knee"; and "We just bit the tip of the iceberg."

Mr. Cunniffe certainly gets my vote for the Tin Ear Award for Free-Style Malapropizing, but he'd better not get complacent; there always are young contenders who are eager to wrest the title away. My friend Lola Battle, a marathon talker in her own diminutive right, offered a dazzling example just last week when she sternly warned her husband (who was ignoring her advice on some important matter) that he was likely to find himself "up a tree without a canoe."

To quote George Burns: "Say goodnight, Gracie."

(10 September 1982)

Thinning Out the Celebrity Diets

Celebrities have a step-over toehold on the publishing business and seem likely to pin it down for the full count. Even those celebrities who are too dull or dimwitted to share with an ever-eager public their secrets on abusive parents, kinky co-stars, recreational sex, or personal triumphs over alcohol and drug abuse are not without ready access to the publishing houses of the world.

Indeed, a quick and sure-fire route to the bestseller list for any celebrity is to offer to their pitiful and perpetually plump public a celebrity diet book.

The market at present is so thoroughly cluttered with these efforts that I have been encouraged by my publishers, Simon & Lipshutz (New York, Philadelphia, and Austell), to permit them to release for commercial distribution a scholarly monograph I recently prepared as a public service entitled "Legislate Against Risky Diets," or, as it is popularly referred to in the scientific community, "LARD."

My study is based on the premise that what seems to be a

great notion from the mouths of celebrities can often have unanticipated and negative results when put into action. With all modesty, I can truthfully say that the study has been widely acclaimed in scientific centers and research institutes throughout the civilized world and in parts of Cobb County.

The meat of the premise is that just because some fruitcake celebrity has an idea, the public should not automatically leap into the conclusion that good will result when pale thought is put to vivid action. By way of historic example, Isadora Duncan, the famous dancer and free-love proponent of the 1920s, once wrote the elderly George Bernard Shaw proposing that they collaborate for the benefit of humanity by producing a child together. "Think what a superior being would result," gushed Ms. Duncan, in the fevered grip of what she believed to be genetic genius, "if we produced a child with your mind and my body."

Shaw (who, to my knowledge, never wrote a celebrity diet book) responded tersely: "I must decline your intriguing offer because there flashed across my mind the horrifying possibility of a child thus produced having *your* mind and *my* body."

The point, obviously, is that many of these highly promoted celebrity diets have severely unfortunate side effects which, prior to the release of my monograph, went entirely unpublicized.

For example, the Jane Fonda Workout Book will, in fact, cause significant weight loss and leave its dedicated followers with body taut as touted. However, the book does not reveal that those who complete the regimen are also left with an uncontrollable urge to marry unsightly radicals and (using the scientific terminology from the monograph) "to speak out relentlessly on public issues they don't know squat about."

There is the Howard Cosell Quick Weight-Loss Diet,

which is successful in producing what he sonorously calls "accelerated avoirdupois minimalization." What his book fails to reveal is that after six weeks on the diet, the skin on one's face becomes so limp and flaccid that the dieter begins to bear an unnerving resemblance to a hung-over bloodhound wearing a cheap toupee.

Of course, all are familiar with the famous Richard Simmons "Light in Your Loafers Quiche and Side-Straddle Hop Regimen," which combines a high concentration of silly disco exercises with a low-fat diet featuring quiche, fruit, and nuts (not to be confused with the small but able San Francisco law firm of the same name). While tests confirm that the diet works, no one has bothered to publicize the inevitable side effects—the dieter winds up with a head that looks like a Q-tip and an overpowering compulsion to wear leotards and skip a lot.

There is the Tip O'Neill "Throwing My Weight Around Diet," which is nothing more than a cunning ploy to mulct a gullible public through promise and intimidation. For $10, the Speaker sends you a 750-calorie-a-day diet and a notarized oath threatening that if you don't follow it to the letter he will come sit on your car.

The Republicans have entered the fray with a Ronald Reagan "Let 'em Eat Cake Diet" (also known as the "We'll Supply Our Side, You Supply Yours Diet"). My monograph treated this entry with thinly veiled disdain, as our tests revealed it was actually no diet at all, but simply a legislative proposal for widespread involuntary fasting.

I wonder what George Bernard Shaw would have said to a proposal to cross Richard Simmons with Tip O'Neill.

(20 October 1982)

Take My Wife, Please

Being a dilettante columnist provokes interesting reactions when confronting readers whom I have not previously met. Invariably, their chief reaction (after noting how much better looking I am in person) is "How do you get away with saying such insensitive things about your wife in the column?"

Such a lack of understanding always astounds me. In the first place, I cannot believe anyone would take anything I say as insensitive toward my wife. In the second place, if by random chance she were to undertake an actual reading of one of my columns, her lips would get tired long before she finished.

In point of fact, there is no real danger that she would ever get up early enough to read a morning newspaper. Even her routine physicals are scheduled in the afternoon, as experience has proven that it is virtually impossible to get a pulse on her before 11:00 a.m.

But, on the larger question of alleged insensitivity, I am always baffled that anyone could find anything I write about my wife to be suspect in that category. Almost every column of mine precipitates an avalanche of letters from college coeds, militant feminists, purple-haired dowagers, and random and admiring stewardesses to the effect that, while I am not as intellectual as Phil Donahue, I am every inch his equal in terms of world-class sensitivity.

Sensitivity is, after all, a relative proposition. Where I grew up, in the wilds of West Georgia, one of my boyhood heroes in Bowdon was the legendary J. D. "Goat" Rankin. He was a paradigm of husbandly sensitivity.

His sensitivity manifested itself in many ways. First and foremost, though he eschewed regular hours and gainful employment for himself, he was always careful to see that his wife had a good job. Furthermore, if his activities at Old Man Paul Morris's Poolroom permitted, he would even pick her up when her factory shift ended so as to get the good woman home in time for her to prepare the evening meal.

I can still remember those late evenings when Goat would rack up his cue and announce, "Boys, I'm going home, and if supper ain't ready I'm going to raise hell, and if it is ready I ain't going to eat it."

One of the best-remembered moments in terms of sensitivity came when our basketball team was playing in the state regionals in LaGrange. A good many Bowdon fans had arranged to be transported to the contest by schoolbus, and Goat had arranged for the bus to stop and pick him up at his bottom-of-the-line Jim Walters home on the south edge of town. When the busload of people pulled into his swept dirt yard, Goat staggered out purposefully, only to be stopped at the door of the bus by his good wife, who, with a number of children hanging to her housedress, said plaintively, "J. D., we don't have any stovewood cut." To which Goat replied, in a tone so soft and suave that it could have issued from Ronald Coleman, "Don't worry, honey, I ain't taking the axe."

With Bowdon as a training ground and J. D. "Goat" Rankin as a role model, it's no wonder that I'm as sensitive as I am.

Before we leave the topic, however, it would be well to point out that those who are most concerned about my wife are those who know her least. Our close friends have long admired my legendary patience with a person they consider to be a wiry, ill-tempered termagant widely known for gratuitously abusing her husband and children. "Faith and begorrah," they often say (particularly those who regularly attend the Barry Fitzgerald Film Festival), "the man's a saint living."

By way of example, I need only cite a recent illustration of her base nature. At a cocktail gathering she and I were accosted by a random and admiring stewardess who, after praising my columns, observed (with amazing acuity for one so young), "I think you're one of the funniest men I know," causing my dour spouse to interject, "You ought to see him without his clothes on." I rest my case.

(10 November 1982)

A Valve Job
for Grizzard

That pulsating star in the modern American literary galaxy, Lewis M. Grizzard (b. Moreland, Georgia, 1946), has just delivered up yet another *tour de force*. His newest book, which has already leaped to the top of the Atlanta Best Sellers List, is an amazing effort.

Amazing, because Grizzard, who is a known University of Georgia graduate, has dazzled literary critics here and abroad by writing sentence after sentence, many of which contain both a noun and a verb.

If that statement appears to reveal a slight bias with respect to the University of Georgia as a citadel of intellectual achievement, I might as well confess it early on. After all, my alma mater, Mercer University, was originally founded as a refuge for those who were too poor to go to Emory and too proud to go to Georgia.

In my college days our Mercer professors convinced us that UGA was nothing more than a hotbed for "mixed dancing" which, as every good Baptist knew, was the cause of severe brain damage. In defense of that position, I should point out that when I made a visit to the University of Georgia library in the mid 1950s it contained only a few books and most of those had already been colored in. Even now (I noted this while reading the yearbook of my scholarly daughter who is currently in residence at that center of learning), the highest academic award in the freshman class at Georgia is the coveted "I Can Dress Myself Badge." But I digress.

Many will be misled by the scholarly title of Grizzard's new book and will doubtless suspect it to be some sort of intellectual piece being republished from the *Kenyon Review*. Titled *They Tore Out My Heart and Stomped That Sucker Flat*, this modern American masterpiece deals principally with affairs of the heart—both clinical and sentimental.

On the clinical side, Grizzard deals in a sensitive fashion with his recent heart surgery. It is a warm and lively tale that will strike a responsive chord in the hearts of anyone who has ever come face to face with a gimlet-eyed surgeon who is about three payments behind on his Mercedes.

On the sentimental side, the much-married Grizzard spins a tale of emotional elation and deflation that would make even Mickey Rooney twitch in unrestrained envy.

It is a book about drama and danger. The greatest drama and danger occurs to the unsuspecting Duroc hog who was ambushed by some Emory orderlies to provide a new heart valve for Grizzard. A sidebar on that story is that the Atlanta Humane Society went to court to get an injunction to prevent Emory from taking the pig's heart valve. When the folks at Emory explained to the Humane Society that the valve was badly needed to replace that of a columnist for the *Atlanta Constitution*, the Humane Society put two more lawyers on the case. Happily for us all the Society lost the case and we got a renewal option on Grizzard and his funniest book to date.

If I have a criticism of the book, it is that Grizzard leaves us hanging as to one of the most important questions raised by his story—what became of the pig whose heart valve they put in Lewis?

At a recent cocktail party an Emory doctor friend of mine revealed to me the true behind-the-scenes answer to this question. What actually happened was that when they put the pig valve in Lewis, they put Lewis's old valve in the pig who, as you might imagine, underwent quite a personality change. The pig has grown a mustache, wears Gucci loafers, neck chains, and open-front shirts, hangs out at singles bars and is now writing a newspaper column under the name of Ron Hudspeth. And now you know . . . the rest of the story.

(19 November 1982)

Yes, It's Me and I'm in Love Again

While drinking a pre-flight toast the other morning to the unsuspecting client who was funding my first class air fare to New York, I was stunned to see Ali MacGraw boarding the plane and taking the seat directly behind mine. By sheer coincidence I had just read an article on Ms. MacGraw in *Interview* magazine the previous weekend and, sensitive soul that I am, was moved to confess to my aging wife that of all the women for whom I would quickly forsake her, Ali MacGraw had long led the list. My wife, unimpressed by my fervent confession, observed that the list had, from time to time, also included Marjorie Main, Minnie Pearl, and the Gish sisters.

Nonetheless, the sight of Ms. MacGraw on Delta 124 in (be still my heart) "the flesh" so fused my mind with concupiscent thoughts that I was, for a fleeting and uncharacteristic moment, speechless.

The sultry Ms. MacGraw, who was accompanied by an aging ex-quarterback named "Frank" or "Fran" Tarklington (or something like that), had been visiting Atlanta in connec-

tion with some gala being staged at that sybaritic watering hole, the Limelight.

Her appearance simply defies calm description—eyes as black and shining as soft bituminous coal, skin as smooth and firm as a perfectly ripe casaba melon, and a willowy and taut figure featuring a pair of industrial strength legs which could easily cause more heart damage than a tank car full of cholesterol. This flawless visage is complemented by the most charming little pearly white front tooth which is endearingly crooked.

Recovering my wits and very, very, casually, I stood up on my seat and turned around to introduce myself. It would be less than honest if I didn't share with you the spark that flashed between us. The quarterback (who must have played for Georgia when they still wore those leather helmets that looked like they should have come with a pair of goggles) was oblivious to Ms. MacGraw's sudden and obvious infatuation with me.

With the legendary dash and verve so characteristic of me, I smoothly engaged her in conversation. We discussed the *Interview* magazine article. We discussed recent books we had both read including *Edie*—I liked it, she liked it, the quarterback said he was "trying to get through" one of Lewis Grizzard's early works but was having trouble with "all those big words." Finally, yielding to the pleas of the surly stewardess who kept insisting that I prepare for flight, I casually strapped the seatbelt across the back of my legs so as to continue our conversation during takeoff.

At length Ms. MacGraw, clearly unable to deal with her feelings for me, ultimately (and I thought very sweetly) broke off our *tête-à-tête* by pretending to go to sleep in the middle of one of my sentences. The old quarterback, who still hadn't caught on, was blissfully engrossed in a copy of *Boy's Life*.

While I certainly don't intend to depart from the code of "A Gentlemen Doesn't Tell," I think I can reveal something of our relationship by describing the parting scene. While the quarterback gabbed with the gaggle of stewardesses who for some reason kept clustering around him (I think he is on some kind of TV show), Ali (by then we had begun to call each other by our first names) took my hand, looked through my eyes and deep into my soul and, in a husky voice which, like it or not, revealed her true and secret thoughts said, "Nice to meet you Paul."

(1 December 1982)

Willie, Jimmy, and Me

There is no sight in the Western world more pitiful than a middle-aged man trying to dress up as something other than a middle-aged man. The unhappy reality of that truism came to me one evening last weekend as I dressed for a Willie Nelson concert.

My carefully coordinated costume consisted of Western-cut bluejeans, of course, topped off with a magnificent cowboy shirt borrowed from my brother who, in his spare time, is a country musician ("The Bullsboro Bluegrass Boys," stars of stage, screen, and Tupperware parties). The shirt was black, fitted and set off with white piping and mother-of-pearl buttons up the front and over the pockets. As I turned in front of my wife's full length mirror I asked, "What Western movie star do I remind you of?" "Well," she reflected as she paused from her arduous routine of applying makeup with a trowel, "the name Smiley Burnett comes to mind." "What's wrong with this look?" I insisted. "Tex," she sniffed, "it's a bit studied."

Crestfallen, I changed back into my standard "lawyer at his

leisure" outfit (heavy on neutral or somber tones of corduroy and Ban-lon) and we went to pick up our friends and fellow Willie Nelson devotees, the Ragsdales. Lawyer Ragsdale, as usual, was in costume appropriate to the occasion but there is something about his appearance that causes him, notwithstanding whatever look he happens to be affecting at the moment, to perpetually resemble a lookout for a massage parlor.

When we reached the Omni I was literally astounded. It looked like a direct hit on the O. K. Corral. Never in recorded history have so many so far East dressed so far West. As far as the eye could see there were young bankers, transmission specialists, Big Star produce managers, insurance salesmen, and auto parts clerks all struggling mightily for a look which could best be characterized as "Charlie Daniels meets the Sons of the Pioneers." My senses were assaulted and dazzled by the feathered cowboy hats, expensive high-heeled boots, Western shirts and kerchiefs, all bobbing in a sea of hooting, howling denim.

Incredibly enough, the only two people I saw during the entire evening that didn't "go Western" were Willie and me. He came on stage in a nondescript T-shirt, baggy blue jogging pants, and docksider moccasins. The only concession he made all evening towards dressing up was to wear, from time to time, one of the myriad hats and kerchiefs that transported fans continued to fling on stage.

Apart from just dressing against type, Nelson is an extraordinary contradiction in many respects. He is a sex symbol to millions of women but if you take a good look at his face you suddenly realize that when Hollywood finally gets around to filming the life story of Gabby Hayes, Willie Nelson has got to play the lead. He is the macho male image for millions of

American men notwithstanding the fact that he wears an earring and does his hair like Veronica Lake. He is an extraordinary musician but for his guitar he prefers a geriatric Martin so old that he has literally picked a hole in it. He is a legendary singer even though his adenoidal Texas twang would make Aubrey Morris of WSB sound like Sir Laurence Olivier by comparison.

Contradictions aside, he lit up the Omni figuratively and literally. After some of his best tunes — "Georgia," "You Were Always on My Mind," "Blue Eyes Crying in the Rain" — the fans showed their appreciation by holding aloft thousands of lighters and matches giving the Omni an eerie, spine-tingling, cathedral effect.

The high point of the evening came when midway through "Amazing Grace" Willie invited on stage a couple of special fans, President and Mrs. Jimmy Carter, who tingled a few spines themselves by singing along.

In all, it was two hours of solid entertainment without one false note. Well, it was almost without one false note. When President Carter came on stage he was wearing street shoes, dress pants, and what appeared to be a denim wrangler jacket, and had a little red bandana tied about his neck. It made one earnestly wish that before leaving for the concert he had asked Rosalyn (who was dressed very stylishly) about his outfit. My guess is that she would have said, "Jimmy, it's a bit studied."

(December 28, 1982)

Special Dedication

To a special friend, Phil Heiner

Love, Friendship Are Life's Absolutes

My friend, Phil Heiner, died of cancer the other morning. At 3:00 a.m. in Piedmont Hospital. Forty-one years old.

Phil was a lawyer, a litigator. He was bright (graduated first in his class at Virginia Law School), mean as hell in court and sweet as could be out of it. He was trim, fit, and good-looking. He was, I thought, a double for actor George Segal— a little taller, but with the same squinty grin and sly good humor. He loved his wife and was proud of and cared deeply for his two children.

Early in the year, with no idea of the ambush in waiting, we were all planning a trip to Greece together. In late March things looked bad, but he was full of fight. In early May he was gone.

As I sat in our kitchen in the still, dark morning of his death, thinking of how to express to his wife the inexpressible, I wondered what meaning there was to his short and grisly struggle. I wanted to think, needed to think, that it revealed something more than the random effect of blind, indifferent chance.

Well, I thought, his horrible battle made us all know he was the man we thought him to be and it revealed to us that we loved him even more than we knew. And his wife's marvelous calm courage and steady devotion offered another ringing example of grace under pressure. But those weren't revelations, just confirmations.

The meaning of the struggle didn't come until I joined a knot of friends at Phil's house just after sunrise. In the awkward atmosphere of those gatherings, where people feel so much but can say so little, Phil's wife gave me a cardboard spiral notebook—a sort of diary he'd been keeping over the three or so months of his illness. The pages were filled with his random scribblings and to me, who had shared with him many good times but no profound thoughts, they were remarkable bits of fight and hope and self-examination. They're worth a moment, especially a moment from the frantic, hard-driving, high-burning, ambitious, young and middle-aged over-achievers:

> There is an overwhelming tendency to denigrate everything I've been able to accomplish in the 'material' world . . . in the rat race. That's not the answer. I have run with the rats and generally finished in the money . . . and if I lick this thing, I'll keep running. That's part of who I am . . . what I am . . . what I believe in. But only part. The soul-searching question is whether (how much?) I have sacrificed the other part.

> When you see success in the mirror and you're impressed with the image, ask how you put it all together and whom you lost by the wayside. Success is relative; love and friends are absolute.

Think about it.

(12 May 1982)

 LUCID INTERVALS

Designed by Haywood Ellis

Composition was by Omni Composition Services, Macon, Georgia
The text was typeset by Joan McCord on an Addressograph/Multigraph
Comp/Set Phototypesetter 5404 in Times Roman (text) and
Avant Garde (display), and paginated on an A/M Comp/Set 4510.

Production specifications:
text paper—60 pound Warren's Olde Style

Printing (offset lithography) by Omnipress of Macon, Inc., Macon, Georgia